Protecting Data in AI

Ethical AI Guide

for

DPO

RAVI RAJPUT

Protecting Data in AI

Ethical AI Guide
for
DPO

RAVI RAJPUT

Introduction

In the digital age, data has become one of the most valuable assets for organizations worldwide. With this rapid growth in data usage comes a responsibility: ensuring that this data is protected, ethically managed, and used in ways that respect individuals' privacy and rights. The role of a Data Protection Officer (DPO) is more critical than ever, especially as artificial intelligence (AI) continues to evolve and become a significant part of our daily lives.

This book delves into the essential role of the Data Protection Officer in the context of AI ethics. Aimed at beginners and those with a foundational understanding of data protection, this guide aims to break down complex concepts and offer practical solutions to common challenges faced by DPOs in the age of AI. We will explore how DPOs can balance the opportunities AI brings with the need to protect personal data, ensuring that organizations use AI responsibly and ethically.

Through real-world examples and clear explanations, this book will help demystify the evolving landscape of data protection in AI and empower DPOs to navigate this complex field. Whether you're just starting your journey in data protection or looking to deepen your knowledge, this book will provide you with the tools, insights, and frameworks to manage AI ethics in data protection successfully.

By the end of this book, you will have a solid understanding of the DPO's responsibilities in AI, the challenges involved, and how to handle these challenges with confidence. Join us in exploring this critical aspect of modern data protection, and learn how to become an effective guardian of privacy and ethics in the age of AI.

Why You Should Read "The Ethical AI Guide for DPO"

In the digital age, artificial intelligence is transforming how we live, work, and interact. But with this innovation comes an increasing need to address the ethical and legal implications of data handling. *The Ethical AI Guide for DPO* is your essential guide to understanding and navigating the complex intersection of AI technology and data protection. This book is not just for experts; it's tailored for beginners and intermediates, empowering you with the knowledge to make a meaningful impact on the way AI systems are designed, managed, and governed. If you're someone looking to understand how data protection officers (DPOs) can shape the ethical framework of AI, this book is a must-read.

The role of a Data Protection Officer has evolved rapidly in the face of AI's growing influence. *The Ethical AI Guide for DPO* delves deep into this transformation, offering clear, actionable strategies for DPOs to navigate their responsibilities in this new era. It's packed with real-world examples and practical guidance, providing you with the tools to address AI-related data breaches, implement robust data protection frameworks, and ensure that ethical considerations are at the forefront of AI development. This book isn't just about theory; it's about preparing you to make real, tangible changes within your organization. Whether you're a DPO, a team member working closely with AI, or someone interested in AI ethics, you'll find invaluable insights to help you lead with integrity and foresight.

As AI continues to reshape industries, the need for responsible and transparent data protection practices has never been more urgent. *The Ethical AI Guide for DPO* equips you with the mindset and skills to rise to these challenges, making sure you're always a step ahead in the evolving regulatory landscape. With the stakes higher than ever, you'll learn how to manage and mitigate risks, safeguard privacy, and protect individuals from potential harm caused by AI technologies. This book ensures that you won't just be reacting to issues—you'll be proactively shaping the future of ethical AI in your organization.

By reading *The Ethical AI Guide for DPO*, you're not just gaining knowledge—you're becoming part of the movement toward more responsible, transparent, and accountable AI systems. This is an opportunity to elevate your career, make a lasting impact in your organization, and contribute to the ethical use of AI across industries. Don't just follow the trends—be the leader who sets them.

About the Author

Ravi Rajput is a seasoned professional with over 24 years of expertise in Information Technology (IT), Information Security, and Operational Technology (OT). His career spans 20+ years in IT and 12+ years in the manufacturing sector, showcasing his ability to bridge the gap between technology and industrial operations.

Ravi holds a degree in Computer Engineering, along with advanced qualifications such as an MSc and an MBA in IT. His credentials are further bolstered by numerous industry certifications across platforms like Microsoft, Cisco, VMware, AWS, and Azure, as well as a prestigious Leadership Certification from Harvard.

In addition to these, Ravi is ISO 22301 - Business Continuity Management System (BCMS) certified Lead Implementer and ISO 27001 - Information Security Management System (ISMS) certified Lead Auditor, further demonstrating his expertise in the critical areas of business continuity and information security.

A passionate advocate for knowledge sharing, Ravi regularly publishes IT articles and delivers impactful talks on topics like IT services, Information Security, and Digital Transformation. His writing reflects his commitment to empowering individuals with knowledge to drive innovation and growth.

Ravi emphasizes the responsible use of data, drawing from his experiences where misuse of information caused harm to individuals and organizations. This has fueled his dedication to educating others on the importance of data awareness.

An active member of CIO and CXO professional networks, Ravi continues to contribute to the broader community through collaboration and thought leadership. Humble yet driven, he is committed to making a meaningful impact by inspiring others and advancing industry practices.

Copyright:

Disclaimer:

This book is intended for informational purposes only. The author and publisher make no representations or warranties with respect to the accuracy or completeness of the contents of this book and disclaim any liability for direct or indirect damages resulting from its use. Examples are provided for better understanding.

Version:01

Date: February 2025

Book Style:

This book combines both theoretical concepts and practical steps, with a focus on real-world application. Multiple examples are provided to enhance understanding, all of which are sourced from the public domain. No claims of ownership are made over these examples, and they are used solely for illustrative purposes.

Along with the above trying to put MOTD (message of the day) for better message and information.

Dedicating The Book

"To my parents, whose unwavering support and guidance have shaped my journey. Your sacrifices have paved the way for my dreams."

"And to my beloved wife, whose love, patience, and encouragement inspire me every day to reach new heights."

Index

8. **Handling Data Breaches in the Age of AI**

   o Common Causes of Data Breaches in AI Systems

   o Procedures for Managing AI Data Breaches

   o Preventative Measures and Best Practices

9. **DPOs and AI Data Ethics in Practice**

   o Real-World Examples of DPOs in AI Ethics Roles

   o Case Studies of AI Implementation and Data Protection Failures

   o Lessons Learned from Successes and Failures

10. **The Future of AI and Data Protection**

    o Trends in AI Development and Data Protection

    o The Evolving Role of the DPO

    o Preparing for the Challenges of Tomorrow

11. **Conclusion and Key Takeaways**

    o Recap of the DPO's Responsibilities in AI Ethics

    o Essential Tools and Mindsets for Success

    o A Call to Action: Leading the Charge in Ethical AI Protection

Table of Contents

Acronyms

DPO: Data Protection Officer

DPIA: Data Protection Impact Assessment

GDPR: General Data Protection Regulation

AI: Artificial Intelligence

NIST: National Institute of Standards and Technology

ISO: International Organization for Standardization

LIME: Local Interpretable Model-agnostic Explanations

SHAP: Shapley Additive Explanations

IBM Fairness 360: IBM's open-source toolkit for detecting and mitigating bias in AI models.

OWASP ZAP: Open Web Application Security Project Zed Attack Proxy, used for penetration testing.

CI/CD: Continuous Integration / Continuous Deployment

H2O.ai: A machine learning platform that automates model training and risk evaluation.

Fiddler AI: A platform for monitoring, explaining, and improving machine learning models.

Prometheus: An open-source system monitoring and alerting toolkit.

FTC: Federal Trade Commission

CCPA: California Consumer Privacy Act

AWS: Amazon Web Services

MFA: Multi-Factor Authentication

IT: Information Technology

ICO: Information Commissioner's Office

PIA: Privacy Impact Assessment

AETHER: AI and Ethics in Engineering and Research Committee

HIPAA: Health Insurance Portability and Accountability Act

EEOC: Equal Employment Opportunity Commission

PIPL: Personal Information Protection Law

OECD: Organisation for Economic Co-operation and Development

CPO: Chief Privacy Officer

EU: European Union

UN: United Nations

Chapter 1: Introduction to Data Protection and AI

1.1 Understanding the Digital Age and Data

The Explosion of Data in the Modern World

In today's digital landscape, the amount of data generated is staggering. Every day, millions of interactions, transactions, and activities across various platforms—social media, e-commerce sites, IoT devices, and more—generate data. This data explosion is primarily driven by the increasing use of digital services, mobile devices, and cloud computing. A report from IDC estimated that by 2025, the global data sphere will reach 175 zettabytes, up from 33 zettabytes in 2018.

The growth of data is both an opportunity and a challenge. It provides businesses with valuable insights into consumer behavior, trends, and preferences, but managing such vast amounts of data requires efficient systems, strong governance, and robust protection mechanisms.

Data as a Currency: How Personal Data Fuels Industries

Personal data has become a vital asset in the modern economy. It powers industries, especially those focused on targeted advertising, customer behavior analytics, and personalized experiences. Companies like Facebook and Google have built multi-billion-dollar empires based largely on the use of personal data, which is sold to advertisers to help them reach specific audiences. The more data a company collects, the better it can predict consumer needs and desires, creating a cycle where data continuously fuels business growth.

For instance, Amazon uses data from customer searches, previous purchases, and browsing behaviors to predict what products an individual might want to buy next, tailoring recommendations accordingly. This personalization increases sales and customer satisfaction.

Real-World Example 1: Facebook (Meta) and Data Usage
Facebook (Meta) uses vast amounts of user data to create targeted ads that help advertisers reach specific demographics. For example, Facebook can track user behavior, such as posts liked, groups joined, and friends made, to personalize ads. This allows advertisers to reach individuals who are most likely to engage with their products. As a result, businesses have seen improved conversion rates, and Facebook has cemented its position as one of the top platforms for digital advertising.
Impact: Businesses can increase their ROI by targeting the right audience, while Facebook continues to grow as a dominant force in online advertising.
Website: www.meta.com

Real-World Example 2: Amazon and Data-Driven Personalization
Amazon's recommendation engine uses data from customers' purchase history, browsing behavior, and ratings to suggest products to users. This data-driven

approach helps increase conversions and customer satisfaction. By analyzing millions of data points, Amazon can make relevant suggestions that often lead to unplanned purchases, boosting their bottom line.

Impact: Amazon's system maximizes both customer satisfaction and business revenue by personalizing the shopping experience based on individual data.

Website: www.amazon.com

The Shift Towards AI and Its Impact on Data Management

With the rise of AI, the way data is managed, analyzed, and used is undergoing a dramatic transformation. AI systems can process vast amounts of data much more efficiently than traditional methods. From predictive analytics to natural language processing, AI is empowering businesses to make data-driven decisions in real-time. However, this also creates new challenges, such as ensuring that AI systems respect privacy, are free from bias, and comply with data protection regulations.

AI can sift through enormous data sets to identify patterns that humans might miss. For example, AI can help health organizations analyze patient data to predict disease outbreaks, or AI-powered chatbots can respond to customer queries instantly by drawing from a pool of historical data.

Checklist for AI and Data Management:

- Ensure AI systems are trained on clean, representative data to avoid biases.
- Regularly audit data collection processes to ensure compliance with data protection laws.
- Implement encryption and other security measures to protect sensitive data.
- Consider user consent and transparency when collecting data for AI systems.

MOTD

"Data is the currency of today's digital world. Manage it well, and the possibilities are endless."

Chapter 1: Introduction to Data Protection and AI
1.2 The Intersection of AI and Data Protection

AI as a Tool for Data Processing

AI has emerged as a powerful tool for processing vast amounts of data quickly and efficiently. Unlike traditional methods that require manual effort or limited automation, AI systems can analyze complex datasets and uncover patterns that might otherwise go unnoticed. Machine learning algorithms can process data, identify trends, and predict future outcomes, all while being trained to improve over time. This ability is transforming industries such as finance, healthcare, and marketing, where the speed and scale of data processing are critical.

For instance, AI-powered algorithms are commonly used in credit scoring systems to evaluate financial data and determine a borrower's risk level. These systems can analyze historical financial records and make predictions in seconds, something that would take a human analyst much longer to do. However, this AI-driven efficiency raises questions about transparency and accountability, especially in sectors that rely heavily on personal and sensitive data.

How AI Creates New Challenges in Data Privacy

While AI offers many advantages, it also introduces new challenges, particularly in data privacy. The more data AI systems have access to, the more they can learn and optimize. However, this creates risks related to over-collection of personal information, lack of consent, and potential misuse of sensitive data.

For example, AI systems might track users' online behavior or interactions without explicitly informing them, which can lead to privacy violations. Algorithms that analyze user data for targeted advertising or content recommendations could inadvertently expose private information if the data isn't handled responsibly.

Real-World Example 1: Google's AI and Data Privacy Concerns
Google uses AI to analyze user data for personalized advertising. While this has enhanced user experience by tailoring ads to specific interests, it has also raised concerns about how much personal information Google collects. Users may unknowingly share more data than they intend to, such as location or browsing history.
Impact: Despite the business growth for Google, privacy advocates have raised red flags about data collection practices and potential misuse.
Website: www.google.com

Real-World Example 2: Health AI and Sensitive Data
In healthcare, AI systems analyze medical data, such as patient records and imaging data, to help doctors diagnose diseases or suggest treatments. For example, IBM's Watson Health uses AI to analyze vast datasets and assist in clinical decision-making. While AI systems improve healthcare outcomes, the handling of sensitive

medical data is highly regulated, and any breach or mishandling can have severe consequences.

Impact: AI improves diagnostic accuracy, but the privacy of patient data remains a critical concern. Companies must ensure compliance with regulations such as HIPAA (Health Insurance Portability and Accountability Act).

Website: www.ibm.com/watson-health

The Need for Responsible Data Handling in AI Systems

With AI's ability to process personal data at scale, there is an urgent need for responsible data handling. Companies must ensure that AI systems are not only effective but also ethical and compliant with privacy laws. This includes obtaining informed consent from individuals before collecting their data, ensuring data is anonymized or pseudonymized where possible, and being transparent about how data is used.

Responsible data handling means implementing robust safeguards to prevent misuse or accidental exposure of personal information. Organizations must integrate privacy considerations throughout the entire AI development lifecycle, from design and data collection to training and deployment.

Checklist for Responsible Data Handling in AI:

- **Data Minimization**: Collect only the data necessary for your AI model's purpose.

- **Informed Consent**: Always obtain user consent before collecting personal data.

- **Data Encryption**: Use encryption methods to protect sensitive data both in transit and at rest.

- **Transparency**: Be transparent with users about how their data will be used and provide them with clear privacy policies.

- **Privacy Audits**: Regularly audit AI systems for compliance with privacy regulations.

MOTD

"Data is powerful, but its responsibility lies in the hands of those who manage it."

Chapter 1: Introduction to Data Protection and AI
1.3 The Growing Need for Ethical Oversight in AI

Ethical Issues in AI: Bias, Transparency, and Accountability

AI technologies are often hailed for their ability to process vast amounts of data and make decisions quickly. However, this efficiency can sometimes come at the cost of fairness, transparency, and accountability. AI systems can perpetuate bias, leading to unfair outcomes, especially when they are trained on skewed or incomplete datasets. For instance, AI-based decision-making systems may unintentionally favor certain demographics while discriminating against others. Bias can creep into AI systems when the data used to train them reflects historical inequalities.

Transparency is another pressing ethical issue. Many AI models, especially deep learning algorithms, are considered "black boxes," meaning that it is often unclear how they arrive at their decisions. Without transparency, it becomes difficult for users to understand why a particular decision was made, raising concerns about accountability when something goes wrong.

Lastly, accountability is a crucial aspect. When an AI system makes a harmful or incorrect decision, it's often unclear who is responsible—whether it's the AI developers, the company deploying the technology, or the AI itself. This ambiguity can create ethical and legal challenges, especially in areas like healthcare, criminal justice, and hiring.

Case Studies of Ethical Failures in AI Systems

1. **Amazon's AI Recruiting Tool**
   In 2018, Amazon scrapped an AI-driven recruitment tool after discovering it was biased against female candidates. The algorithm, which was designed to help Amazon automate hiring processes, showed a preference for male candidates over female ones, primarily because it had been trained on resumes submitted to Amazon over the past ten years—most of which came from men.
   Impact: The incident highlighted the risks of bias in AI training data and the potential consequences of deploying AI systems without proper ethical oversight.
   Website: www.amazon.com

2. **COMPAS Algorithm in Criminal Justice**
   In the U.S., the COMPAS (Correctional Offender Management Profiling for Alternative Sanctions) algorithm was used to assess the likelihood of re-offending by criminals. However, investigations revealed that the algorithm was biased against African American defendants, overestimating their risk of recidivism. This raised questions about fairness and transparency in criminal justice AI systems.
   Impact: The case underlined the critical need for ethical audits in AI systems,

especially in sectors like criminal justice, where biased algorithms can have life-altering consequences.
Website: www.propublica.org

The Importance of Establishing Ethical Guidelines for AI

With AI's growing influence, the need for ethical guidelines has never been more urgent. Ethical guidelines in AI development can help ensure that AI systems are designed to promote fairness, transparency, and accountability. By establishing clear ethical frameworks, organizations can reduce the risks of bias and discrimination while ensuring that their AI models are interpretable and accountable.

AI ethics guidelines should focus on:

- **Bias Mitigation**: Ensuring AI systems are trained on diverse datasets to minimize bias.

- **Transparency**: Building explainable AI models that allow users to understand how decisions are made.

- **Accountability**: Defining clear accountability structures for decisions made by AI systems.

- **Continuous Monitoring**: Regularly auditing AI systems to ensure they adhere to ethical guidelines throughout their lifecycle.

Checklist for Ethical AI Design:

- **Bias Detection**: Regularly test AI models for bias, especially when dealing with sensitive sectors like hiring or criminal justice.

- **Explainability**: Ensure that AI decisions can be explained in human terms, especially for high-stakes decisions.

- **Stakeholder Engagement**: Involve diverse stakeholders, including ethicists and social scientists, in the design of AI systems.

- **Audit and Accountability**: Implement a system for auditing AI decisions and assign clear accountability when issues arise.

MOTD

"Ethical AI is not a luxury; it's a necessity for building a fairer, more transparent future."

Chapter 1: Introduction to Data Protection and AI
1.4 The DPO's Role in AI Ethics

Key Responsibilities of the DPO in the AI Landscape

The Data Protection Officer (DPO) plays a pivotal role in ensuring that AI technologies are developed, deployed, and maintained in a manner that respects data privacy rights. As organizations leverage AI to drive business innovation, the DPO must ensure that AI systems are compliant with data protection laws such as the General Data Protection Regulation (GDPR). Key responsibilities include:

- **Data Protection Impact Assessments (DPIAs)**: The DPO should ensure that a DPIA is conducted for any AI system that processes sensitive personal data. This assessment helps identify potential risks related to data processing and ensure that privacy risks are mitigated.

- **Compliance Monitoring**: The DPO is responsible for monitoring AI systems to ensure they remain in compliance with privacy laws throughout their lifecycle, especially when AI systems evolve or new features are introduced.

- **Advisory Role**: The DPO serves as an advisor to the organization, guiding leadership on how to implement AI projects that align with privacy laws and ethical considerations.

How the DPO Helps Balance Innovation with Privacy

AI and data-driven innovation often involve processing vast amounts of personal data. The DPO's role is critical in ensuring that privacy considerations do not impede technological advancement. By helping organizations strike a balance between AI innovation and privacy protection, the DPO ensures that:

- **Privacy by Design**: Privacy protection is embedded into the AI development process from the start, ensuring that data privacy is not an afterthought.

- **Minimization of Data**: The DPO ensures that AI systems only collect the minimum amount of personal data necessary for their purpose, reducing potential privacy risks.

- **Transparency**: The DPO helps ensure that organizations are transparent about their data practices, clearly communicating with users how their data will be used in AI systems.

The DPO as the Gatekeeper of Ethical AI Practices

The DPO plays a crucial role in maintaining the ethical integrity of AI systems. As gatekeepers of data protection, DPOs ensure that AI systems adhere to ethical principles such as fairness, transparency, and accountability. This includes:

- **Bias Mitigation**: Ensuring that AI models do not perpetuate or amplify existing biases in data.

- **Data Sovereignty**: Overseeing how data is collected, stored, and processed, ensuring that it respects the rights of individuals and complies with data protection laws.

- **Ensuring Accountability**: The DPO helps establish accountability frameworks, ensuring that the organization is responsible for any ethical or privacy-related issues that arise from AI deployment.

Real-World Examples

1. **The Role of DPO in Healthcare AI**
   In the healthcare industry, AI applications like predictive analytics or patient data processing systems require stringent data protection measures. A DPO at a hospital or health tech company ensures that AI algorithms, which analyze patient data, comply with data privacy regulations such as GDPR or HIPAA.
   Impact: The DPO ensures that personal health data is processed in a way that protects patients' privacy and rights while also enabling the use of AI for medical innovations like early disease detection.
   Website: www.hipaajournal.com

2. **Google's AI Principles and DPO Oversight**
   Google introduced AI principles in 2018 that outlined how the company would use AI responsibly. A DPO at Google would be essential in ensuring these principles are followed, balancing the push for innovation with the protection of user data and privacy.
   Impact: Google's DPO ensures that AI-powered products, such as Google Assistant, respect user privacy and comply with data protection regulations. This oversight prevents potential violations of user rights while allowing AI systems to evolve.
   Website: www.blog.google

Checklist for DPOs Managing AI Ethics:

- **Conduct DPIAs for AI Projects**: Ensure that any new AI initiative undergoes a Data Protection Impact Assessment.

- **Monitor AI Systems for Compliance**: Continuously audit AI systems for compliance with data protection laws.

- **Promote Privacy by Design**: Ensure that privacy is embedded into the development of all AI systems.

- **Ensure Bias Mitigation**: Regularly test AI algorithms for fairness and mitigate any discovered biases.

- **Establish Accountability Structures**: Define who is accountable for AI decisions and ensure transparency in decision-making processes.

MOTD

"AI innovation can thrive, but only when balanced with privacy and ethical responsibility."

Chapter 1: Introduction to Data Protection and AI
1.5 Overview of the Book Structure

Breakdown of the Chapters and the Journey Ahead

This book is structured to guide you step-by-step through the intricacies of data protection, ethical AI practices, and the critical role of the Data Protection Officer (DPO). Each chapter builds on the last, laying a solid foundation for understanding the complex landscape of AI and data protection.

1. **Chapter 1: Introduction to Data Protection and AI** – You've just started the journey. This chapter sets the stage for understanding the digital age, how AI intersects with data protection, and why ethical oversight is crucial.

2. **Chapter 2: The Role of the Data Protection Officer (DPO)** – Here, we dive deep into what a DPO does, their responsibilities, and the skills they need to thrive in the age of AI.

3. **Chapter 3: AI and Data Privacy: A New Frontier** – This chapter explores how AI uses personal data and the risks it creates for privacy, setting the stage for the ethical frameworks discussed in later chapters.

4. **Chapter 4: The Ethical Dimensions of AI** – Now, we turn to the ethical challenges AI presents, discussing issues like bias, fairness, and accountability.

5. **Chapter 5: Legal Frameworks and Regulations Affecting DPOs** – This chapter looks at laws and regulations, such as GDPR, that every DPO must navigate when working with AI technologies.

6. **Chapters 6-10** – The next chapters dive into practical aspects, like risk management, transparency, and handling data breaches, giving real-world tools and techniques for DPOs working with AI.

How Each Chapter Builds on the Other

As you progress through the book, you'll notice that each chapter naturally builds on the previous one. For example, Chapter 2 introduces you to the DPO's role, and Chapter 3 then explores the implications of that role in the context of AI. Legal frameworks discussed in Chapter 5 become more meaningful when you understand the risks and ethical dilemmas from earlier chapters. Each section will empower you with the knowledge needed to make informed decisions as a DPO in the AI era.

Key Takeaways from the Book

By the end of the book, you will:

- Gain a deep understanding of the DPO's essential role in AI projects.

- Learn how to navigate the intersection of AI and data protection.

- Develop practical tools for ensuring ethical, transparent, and compliant AI systems.

- Understand how to balance innovation with privacy, and how to act as an advocate for ethical AI practices in your organization.

Real-World Examples

1. **The European Union's GDPR**
   The GDPR is a cornerstone regulation that impacts how AI systems handle personal data. The DPO plays a key role in ensuring that AI-driven projects comply with GDPR's principles of transparency, accountability, and data minimization.
   Impact: GDPR compliance prevents privacy violations and helps companies avoid heavy fines, encouraging ethical AI practices.
   Website: www.eugdpr.org

2. **AI in Autonomous Vehicles (Waymo)**
   Waymo, Google's self-driving car division, collects massive amounts of data to train its AI algorithms. A DPO in this scenario ensures that data collection practices respect user privacy and comply with data protection laws.
   Impact: DPOs help manage the ethical use of data, ensuring that personal information isn't misused, fostering public trust in autonomous technology.
   Website: www.waymo.com

Checklist for Following the Book's Structure

- **Track Progress**: As you move through each chapter, take note of how each section connects with the previous one.

- **Reflect on Key Takeaways**: After each chapter, pause and consider how the insights apply to your own role or organization.

- **Act on Action Points**: Implement the action points at the end of each section to stay aligned with the book's goals.

MOTD

"Mastering the intersection of AI and data protection is a journey, not a destination. Stay focused, stay curious!"

Chapter 2: The Role of the Data Protection Officer (DPO)

2.1 What Does a DPO Do?

Core Responsibilities of a DPO in Any Organization

The Data Protection Officer (DPO) is a pivotal role in any organization that handles personal data. At its core, a DPO ensures that data protection regulations are followed, mitigating risks related to privacy breaches. The key responsibilities include:

1. **Ensuring Legal Compliance**: A DPO must ensure that the organization complies with data protection laws such as GDPR, CCPA, and others applicable based on the region or industry. They guide the organization on legal obligations, advising on what data can be processed, how it should be stored, and for how long.

2. **Data Protection Impact Assessments (DPIAs)**: The DPO conducts regular assessments to evaluate the risks of processing personal data and ensures that privacy risks are addressed before projects or technologies are deployed.

3. **Staff Training and Awareness**: A DPO is responsible for training staff on data protection and privacy issues, ensuring that the organization's workforce is well-aware of the importance of safeguarding personal data.

4. **Providing Expert Advice**: The DPO provides expert advice on data protection issues, helping the organization understand complex legal and ethical guidelines and how they translate into day-to-day operations.

Monitoring Compliance with Data Protection Laws

A critical part of the DPO's role is ensuring that the organization's practices align with legal standards. This includes:

- **Auditing Data Handling Practices**: The DPO ensures that data is processed securely, minimizing risks of unauthorized access, data loss, or breaches.

- **Reviewing Contracts**: The DPO often reviews third-party contracts to ensure that third parties comply with the same data protection standards.

Acting as a Liaison Between Stakeholders and Regulators

The DPO acts as the main point of contact for both internal and external stakeholders regarding data protection. This involves:

- **Internal Liaison**: Acting as the go-to expert for data protection issues across various departments like HR, IT, and Marketing.

- **External Liaison**: Representing the organization during audits or investigations by regulatory authorities such as the Information Commissioner's Office (ICO) or European Data Protection Board (EDPB).

Action Point

Map out the primary duties of a DPO in your organization. Whether you are currently in the role or just beginning to understand it, identify key areas where your organization can improve compliance and awareness around data protection. Consider creating a checklist to track ongoing compliance activities and responsibilities.

Real-World Examples

1. **Microsoft's Chief Privacy Officer (CPO)**
   Microsoft has a dedicated CPO responsible for ensuring compliance with global privacy laws like GDPR and CCPA. By establishing a dedicated team under the CPO's leadership, Microsoft can proactively address privacy issues and monitor compliance across their global operations.
   Impact: Microsoft has built a strong reputation for privacy, especially in their cloud business, gaining the trust of customers and regulators alike.
   Website: www.microsoft.com/privacy

2. **Google and GDPR Compliance**
   Google's DPO ensures that the company's operations comply with the GDPR by overseeing how data is processed across its advertising, cloud, and other services. Their DPO team works closely with regulators to ensure that Google's policies are always up-to-date with the latest privacy regulations.
   Impact: Google has avoided several fines by maintaining a proactive and transparent data protection strategy.
   Website: www.google.com/privacy

Checklist for the DPO's Primary Duties

- **Ensure GDPR compliance**: Review data processing activities, storage, and retention policies regularly.

- **Conduct DPIAs**: Evaluate and address potential privacy risks in projects.

- **Engage with legal teams**: Review contracts and third-party agreements for data protection compliance.

- **Monitor data protection practices**: Conduct regular internal audits to ensure data security measures are up to date.

- **Educate staff**: Implement regular training programs for employees on privacy and security issues.

MOTD

"Data protection isn't just a legal requirement—it's a strategic advantage that builds trust and drives success."

Chapter 2: The Role of the Data Protection Officer (DPO)
2.2 Key Responsibilities and Skills Required

Knowledge of Data Protection Laws and Regulations

A Data Protection Officer (DPO) must possess a comprehensive understanding of data protection laws and regulations, as these form the bedrock of their daily responsibilities. This includes knowledge of:

- **General Data Protection Regulation (GDPR)**: The DPO should be familiar with the nuances of the GDPR, its principles, and requirements such as data subject rights, lawful bases for processing, and data breach notification.

- **Other Regional Laws**: Depending on the region, a DPO may need to understand additional laws such as the California Consumer Privacy Act (CCPA) or the Personal Data Protection Act (PDPA) in Singapore. These laws may differ in terms of their implementation but still share a common focus on protecting individuals' data.

- **International Standards**: A DPO working for global companies should also be aware of international regulations and frameworks, such as the EU-US Privacy Shield or the APEC Privacy Framework.

Analytical Thinking and Risk Management Skills

A key skill for a DPO is the ability to think analytically about data privacy and security risks. This includes:

- **Data Protection Impact Assessments (DPIAs)**: The DPO must assess the privacy risks associated with new projects, technologies, or business activities. They must identify potential threats to data security and recommend strategies to mitigate these risks.

- **Risk Mitigation**: The DPO plays a significant role in designing and implementing risk management strategies. This may involve setting up data encryption methods, recommending security measures for data storage, and guiding the organization on how to handle data subject requests efficiently.

Communication and Negotiation Skills

A DPO acts as the bridge between the organization, regulators, and data subjects, so strong communication skills are essential:

- **Internal Communication**: The DPO should be able to clearly communicate complex legal and technical data protection topics to non-expert stakeholders (e.g., senior management, IT teams).

- **External Communication**: The DPO may need to represent the organization during audits, investigations, or legal proceedings. Negotiating with regulators and stakeholders about compliance requirements is also a crucial skill.

Action Point

Assess your current skill set or gaps as a DPO. Take a moment to reflect on where you might need to expand your knowledge or strengthen your abilities, particularly in the areas of legal knowledge, analytical thinking, and communication. Consider taking professional courses, attending workshops, or reading key privacy-related publications to deepen your expertise.

Real-World Examples

1. **Facebook's Privacy Team**
   Facebook's Chief Privacy Officer and team are responsible for ensuring compliance with global data protection regulations. Their deep knowledge of the GDPR and other laws allows Facebook to adjust its data processing practices proactively, minimizing the risk of legal issues.
   Impact: Facebook's strong legal expertise helps mitigate the risk of high-profile data breach fines, as seen during their successful handling of GDPR audits.
   Website: www.facebook.com/privacy

2. **Apple's Commitment to Privacy**
   Apple has invested heavily in both its privacy policies and its DPO's ability to communicate these policies clearly to the public and regulators. Apple's DPO team works diligently to ensure that data processing practices are transparent and comply with all relevant privacy laws.
   Impact: Apple's approach has built consumer trust, positioning the company as a leader in privacy protection, especially in contrast to competitors.
   Website: www.apple.com/privacy

Checklist for DPO Skills Assessment

- **Legal Knowledge**: Have I reviewed and understood the key provisions of GDPR and other data protection regulations relevant to my role?

- **Risk Management**: Do I have a clear process in place for assessing and mitigating data protection risks?

- **Communication Skills**: Am I able to explain complex data protection issues in a clear and accessible way to various stakeholders?

- **Ongoing Learning**: Am I continuously improving my knowledge and skills through training or certifications?

MOTD

"Continuous learning in data protection makes you not just compliant, but a true privacy advocate."

Chapter 2: The Role of the Data Protection Officer (DPO)
2.3 Legal and Ethical Foundations of the DPO's Role

Legal Responsibilities Under GDPR and Other Laws

A Data Protection Officer (DPO) is entrusted with ensuring that an organization complies with data protection laws, the most prominent being the **General Data Protection Regulation (GDPR)**. The DPO's legal responsibilities include:

- **Monitoring Compliance**: The DPO is responsible for ensuring that the organization complies with the requirements of GDPR, such as conducting Data Protection Impact Assessments (DPIAs), ensuring that data subjects' rights are respected, and overseeing data breach response protocols.

- **Record-Keeping and Reporting**: Under GDPR, DPOs must maintain records of data processing activities, which are subject to audit by regulatory bodies. The DPO also serves as the point of contact for data protection authorities and must report any breaches.

- **Facilitating Data Subject Rights**: The DPO ensures that individuals' rights to access, rectify, or erase their data are respected, and that the organization responds to these requests in a timely manner.

In addition to GDPR, the DPO must be familiar with other relevant laws such as the **California Consumer Privacy Act (CCPA)** or the **Personal Data Protection Act (PDPA)** in Singapore, which may introduce different legal requirements for data privacy.

The Ethical Standards DPOs Should Uphold

Beyond legal requirements, the DPO must uphold strong **ethical standards**. These include:

- **Transparency**: The DPO should ensure the organization is transparent with users about data collection, processing, and sharing practices. Ethical data usage means not only complying with the law but also building trust with data subjects.

- **Accountability**: The DPO must ensure that the organization is accountable for the data it processes, including maintaining appropriate data protection measures, and that it can demonstrate its compliance with laws and ethical standards.

- **Fairness**: Ethical DPOs ensure that data collection and processing activities are done fairly, not taking advantage of vulnerable individuals or groups.

Navigating Between Legal Compliance and Ethical Considerations

The DPO often faces complex decisions where legal requirements may not completely align with ethical considerations. For example, while an organization may be legally allowed to process certain personal data, doing so may be perceived as an invasion of privacy. The DPO's role is to strike a balance between these two forces.

- **Case in Point**: In situations where consent is ambiguous or difficult to obtain, the DPO must decide whether to proceed with data collection based on legal grounds, or find an ethical solution to gain more transparency and consent from individuals.

- **Example**: In the case of **Google's "Project Nightingale"**, where Google was collecting health data from millions of individuals without proper consent, the DPO's involvement would have been crucial in ensuring not just legal compliance but also ethical handling of sensitive personal data.

Action Point

Build a framework for legal and ethical decision-making in your organization. Start by identifying potential risks where legal and ethical concerns may diverge. Ensure your framework is based on transparency, fairness, and accountability, and apply it to situations where data processing practices could be questioned by stakeholders.

Real-World Examples

1. **Cambridge Analytica Scandal (2018)**
   The infamous data misuse case saw Cambridge Analytica harvesting data from millions of Facebook users without their informed consent. The DPOs involved failed to navigate both the legal compliance with GDPR and the ethical implications of using data for targeted political ads.
   Impact: It resulted in widespread public backlash, regulatory fines, and significant damage to Facebook's reputation.
   Website: www.theguardian.com

2. **Microsoft's Privacy by Design**
   Microsoft is a prime example of an organization that integrates legal compliance with ethical standards. Microsoft's approach to privacy and data protection emphasizes transparency, consumer choice, and fairness. The company has implemented rigorous internal policies, ensuring that privacy is an integral part of every product from the outset.
   Impact: Their ethical data practices have garnered trust from users and regulators alike, positioning them as a leader in privacy protection.
   Website: www.microsoft.com/privacy

Checklist for Building a Legal & Ethical Framework

- **Legal Compliance**: Have I reviewed all relevant laws (GDPR, CCPA, etc.) to understand my legal obligations?

- **Ethical Principles**: Have I established clear ethical guidelines for data collection and processing (e.g., transparency, fairness, accountability)?

- **Risk Assessment**: Do I regularly assess potential conflicts between legal requirements and ethical concerns in data protection?

- **Stakeholder Engagement**: Am I engaging with internal and external stakeholders to ensure ethical data practices are upheld?

MOTD

"Ethical decisions build trust, while legal compliance ensures stability—together, they form the foundation of data protection."

Chapter 2: The Role of the Data Protection Officer (DPO)
2.4 The DPO's Role in AI Development

How DPOs Guide AI Systems Toward Ethical Use of Data

As artificial intelligence (AI) increasingly relies on vast datasets, the DPO plays a crucial role in ensuring that the AI systems developed within an organization follow ethical guidelines when it comes to handling personal data. DPOs should oversee that AI algorithms do not infringe upon individuals' rights or privacy. This includes ensuring:

- **Informed Consent**: AI systems often require large datasets that may contain personal information. The DPO ensures that the data is collected transparently and with the explicit consent of individuals where necessary.

- **Bias Mitigation**: AI systems can inadvertently perpetuate biases, especially if the data used to train them is not diverse or is skewed. The DPO's role is to guide the development team in ensuring the AI system is fair and does not discriminate against certain groups.

Monitoring AI Technologies for Data Privacy Compliance

AI systems, by nature, continuously evolve and process vast amounts of data, which creates ongoing privacy concerns. The DPO's responsibility is to monitor these technologies and ensure they comply with data protection laws like the GDPR. This includes:

- **Data Minimization**: Ensuring that AI systems only collect and use the minimum amount of data necessary to perform their function.

- **Data Security**: AI systems must be designed with data security in mind, and the DPO must monitor the implementation of measures that protect personal data from unauthorized access and breaches.

- **Right to Explanation**: DPOs need to ensure that individuals can understand how AI algorithms use their data, especially when decisions are made about them (e.g., credit scoring, hiring processes).

Collaboration with AI Developers and Legal Teams

The DPO should work closely with both the **AI development team** and the **legal team** to create a robust data protection framework. This collaboration is essential to ensure that privacy and ethical considerations are built into the AI system from the ground up:

- **AI Design**: The DPO helps the AI development team ensure that data protection principles such as privacy by design are incorporated early in the development phase. This ensures that privacy features are not an afterthought but an integral part of the system.

- **Legal Compliance**: Collaborating with the legal team helps ensure that all data collection and processing activities related to AI are in compliance with relevant data protection laws, such as GDPR or CCPA.

Action Point

Integrate data protection principles early in the AI development cycle. Engage with developers, legal teams, and other relevant stakeholders to ensure that privacy and ethical concerns are considered from the design phase, not just during deployment.

Real-World Examples

1. **IBM Watson and Healthcare Data**
   IBM Watson Health is a prime example of AI used in the healthcare sector, where large amounts of personal health data are processed. IBM has faced scrutiny over privacy concerns, particularly regarding the use of sensitive medical data in training AI algorithms. The company's DPOs were key in establishing protocols to ensure that the data used was anonymized and compliant with healthcare privacy regulations like HIPAA.
   Impact: The focus on ethical use of data helped IBM build trust with healthcare providers and patients, ensuring that AI was used responsibly in life-altering decisions.
   Website: www.ibm.com/watson-health

2. **Google DeepMind Health**
   Google's DeepMind Health project faced scrutiny in 2017 when it was revealed that data from 1.6 million patients was used without proper consent. In response, Google appointed a DPO to monitor the AI project and ensure better transparency in the collection and usage of health data. This intervention led to more stringent consent protocols and better collaboration with regulators.
   Impact: The action taken by the DPO led to improved public perception and trust in DeepMind's data practices and reinforced the importance of ethical oversight in AI development.
   Website: www.deepmind.com

Checklist for Integrating Data Protection in AI Development

- **Data Minimization**: Have I ensured that the AI system only processes the minimal amount of personal data necessary for its function?

- **Bias Checks**: Is there a procedure in place to check for biases in the AI's decision-making process?

- **Privacy by Design**: Have I ensured that privacy is a consideration at the earliest stages of the AI development process?

- **Transparency**: Can individuals easily understand how their data is being used and processed by AI?

- **Ongoing Monitoring**: Is there a system in place for continuous monitoring and auditing of the AI system to ensure it remains compliant with data protection regulations?

MOTD

"Building ethical AI begins with protecting the data—it's not just compliance; it's trust in action."

Chapter 2: The Role of the Data Protection Officer (DPO)
2.5 Challenges Faced by DPOs in AI

1. Balancing AI Innovation with Data Protection Standards

AI is a rapidly evolving field, and its capacity to innovate seems limitless. However, this innovation can sometimes conflict with data protection standards that demand strict controls over how personal data is collected, stored, and used. DPOs are tasked with striking a balance between fostering innovation—such as enabling AI-powered products and services—and ensuring that these innovations comply with data protection laws like GDPR. This includes:

- **Data Minimization**: Ensuring that AI systems do not collect more data than necessary.

- **Anonymization**: Encouraging the use of anonymized datasets for AI training to protect personal information while still allowing AI to function effectively.

- **Innovation within Boundaries**: Guiding the development teams to build AI solutions that are innovative but do not cross the line of privacy infringement.

This balancing act is often difficult as some AI applications, like facial recognition or predictive analytics, require vast amounts of personal data to work efficiently, which may challenge the DPO's efforts to maintain privacy standards.

2. Dealing with Constantly Evolving Regulations and Technologies

The legal landscape for AI and data protection is constantly changing. DPOs face the challenge of staying updated on new data protection laws (such as GDPR, CCPA) and how they apply to AI. Meanwhile, technology is evolving rapidly, and new AI techniques, tools, and applications emerge frequently. The DPO needs to:

- **Continuous Learning**: Keep up with global and local regulations regarding AI, including recent regulatory changes like the EU's AI Act.

- **Adapting to Technological Changes**: Ensure that new AI developments do not outpace regulatory frameworks and that compliance requirements are met.

This is a particularly difficult challenge as the regulation of AI lags behind its technological development. The DPO must often navigate uncharted legal territory, requiring adaptability and proactive decision-making.

3. Addressing Public Concerns Around AI and Privacy

Public trust in AI technologies is fragile, particularly when it comes to the collection and processing of personal data. DPOs must manage this concern, ensuring that AI systems are transparent, explainable, and secure, while also educating the public and building trust. Some key tasks include:

- **Transparency**: Clearly communicating to the public how AI systems use their data.

- **Accountability**: Ensuring that organizations take responsibility when AI systems cause harm or violate privacy rights.

- **Engaging with Stakeholders**: Having open discussions about the ethical use of AI and reassuring individuals that their data is secure.

By addressing public concerns head-on, DPOs not only protect the organization from reputational risks but also contribute to the broader social responsibility of ethical AI usage.

Action Point

Prepare for the future challenges of data protection in AI by continuously updating your knowledge of emerging technologies, monitoring regulatory changes, and developing strategies to address public concerns around AI and privacy. Build a flexible framework that allows for rapid response to regulatory changes while maintaining high data protection standards.

Real-World Examples

1. **Cambridge Analytica Scandal**
   The Cambridge Analytica scandal (2018) highlighted the dangers of mishandling personal data, particularly in AI-driven marketing and political campaigning. Facebook's data privacy practices were found to be deeply flawed, allowing third-party companies to harvest personal data without consent. The impact was devastating, not only leading to public outrage but also to a $5 billion fine for Facebook by the Federal Trade Commission (FTC). The role of the DPO in managing such risks would have been crucial in ensuring that data was collected ethically and securely.
   Impact: This case underscored the importance of strong data protection practices, especially for AI systems using personal data for profiling.
   Website: Cambridge Analytica Scandal Details

2. **Clearview AI and Facial Recognition**
   Clearview AI is a facial recognition company that scraped images from social media platforms to train its AI algorithms without consent from the individuals. Clearview AI faced significant backlash, with many questioning the ethical implications of using AI in this manner. Multiple lawsuits and privacy concerns were raised, highlighting the challenges DPOs face in ensuring compliance with privacy laws when dealing with cutting-edge AI technologies.
   Impact: This case illustrates how unchecked AI innovations, especially in sensitive areas like facial recognition, can lead to public distrust and legal consequences.
   Website: Clearview AI Controversy

Checklist for DPOs to Overcome AI Challenges

- **Stay Informed**: Regularly review and update knowledge on evolving data protection laws and AI technologies.

- **Integrate Privacy by Design**: Collaborate with AI teams to ensure that privacy is a fundamental part of the development process.

- **Create Transparency Protocols**: Establish clear guidelines for how AI systems should disclose data usage to the public.

- **Risk Mitigation**: Develop strategies to address public concerns proactively and ensure AI systems are ethical and compliant.

- **Regular Audits**: Conduct periodic audits of AI systems to ensure compliance with both ethical and legal standards.

MOTD

"Facing challenges head-on builds the foundation for responsible, innovative AI—embrace the journey of ethical data protection!"

Chapter 3: AI and Data Privacy: A New Frontier

3.1 How AI Utilizes Personal Data

1. AI's Role in Analyzing and Processing Vast Datasets

Artificial intelligence excels at processing large amounts of data that would overwhelm human analysts. AI systems can sift through vast datasets to identify patterns, make predictions, and automate decision-making. This capability allows businesses to derive insights from datasets that might otherwise remain untapped. AI can help identify trends in consumer behavior, predict market movements, or even detect fraud.

- **Practical Advice**: If you work in a data-driven organization, map out how your AI systems collect, analyze, and store data. Understanding this flow ensures you can manage and safeguard it effectively.

For instance, AI-powered recommendation engines, like those used by Netflix or Amazon, analyze past customer interactions to recommend movies, products, or services. These systems process millions of data points to predict the next best action for a user, demonstrating the power of AI to transform user engagement.

2. The Types of Data Used by AI: From Behavioral Data to Sensitive Data

AI utilizes a wide array of personal data to function, including:

- **Behavioral Data**: This includes information about individuals' browsing habits, purchasing behavior, and interactions with digital platforms. Companies like Google and Facebook collect this data to target ads and personalize user experiences.

- **Sensitive Data**: This includes health information, biometric data, or financial data. For instance, AI used in healthcare applications can process medical records to provide predictive diagnostics.

However, as AI systems use more sensitive data, they pose risks to privacy. For example, facial recognition technology uses biometric data, raising concerns about consent and misuse.

- **Practical Advice**: Ensure that the AI systems in your organization are compliant with data protection laws like GDPR, which restricts the collection of sensitive data unless there's explicit consent.

3. The Implications of Data-Driven Decision-Making in AI

AI systems influence many decisions, from the credit scores that determine loan eligibility to the algorithms that determine job candidate suitability. These AI-powered decisions can significantly impact individuals' lives and raise ethical concerns.

- **Bias and Fairness**: AI decision-making systems can inadvertently perpetuate biases if the data used to train them is skewed or incomplete. For example, an AI model trained on biased historical hiring data might discriminate against certain demographic groups, leading to unethical outcomes.

- **Practical Advice**: Regularly audit AI models for fairness and transparency. Implement a "bias detection" mechanism to monitor and correct any biases that may creep into the decision-making process.

Action Point

Understand the data flows in your organization's AI systems by documenting the types of data collected, how it's processed, and where it's stored. Regularly assess data usage to ensure compliance with data privacy regulations and ethical standards.

Real-World Examples

1. **Amazon's Hiring Algorithm**
   Amazon's AI-powered recruitment tool was designed to automate and streamline hiring by analyzing resumes and recommending candidates. However, the system showed bias against female candidates because it had been trained primarily on resumes submitted to Amazon in previous years, which were predominantly from men. This led to a problematic bias in the decision-making process. Amazon eventually scrapped the tool.
   Impact: This is a stark example of how data-driven decision-making in AI can result in discrimination if the data used is not diverse or properly vetted.
   Website: Amazon AI Recruitment Bias

2. **Google's Health Data Controversy (Project Nightingale)**
   In 2019, Google partnered with Ascension, one of the largest healthcare providers in the U.S., to collect and analyze patients' health data under Project Nightingale. This initiative aimed to develop AI models that would improve healthcare. However, it was revealed that millions of Americans' health records were transferred without their knowledge or consent. The controversy centered on how sensitive data was being used by AI without proper transparency.
   Impact: This case highlights the ethical implications of using sensitive personal data without proper consent or transparency in AI applications. It emphasizes the need for ethical oversight when AI systems process personal health information.
   Website: Google Project Nightingale Controversy

Checklist for DPOs to Ensure Ethical AI Data Use

- **Data Flow Mapping**: Identify where data originates, how it's processed, and where it's stored in AI systems.

- **Data Minimization**: Ensure only necessary data is collected for AI operations.

- **Bias Monitoring**: Regularly test AI models for fairness and bias.

- **Transparency**: Maintain clear documentation about AI's data usage and provide transparency to the public.

- **Compliance Audits**: Ensure AI systems comply with local and international data privacy regulations.

MOTD

"Data powers AI, but responsibility powers trust—make sure both work in harmony."

Chapter 3: AI and Data Privacy: A New Frontier
3.2 Privacy Risks in AI-Driven Systems

1. Data Misuse, Breaches, and Unintended Consequences

AI systems often rely on vast amounts of personal data to generate insights and automate decisions. However, this extensive use of data opens up opportunities for misuse, breaches, and unintended consequences:

- **Data Misuse**: AI can inadvertently misuse personal data if the model isn't designed with proper safeguards. For instance, a recommendation engine might use personal browsing history or sensitive personal information in ways the user did not expect or consent to, leading to privacy violations.

- **Data Breaches**: AI systems often require centralized data storage, making them prime targets for hackers. If AI models are not adequately secured, they could expose large datasets containing personal information. A breach in AI systems can lead to identity theft, financial loss, and other serious consequences for affected individuals.

- **Unintended Consequences**: AI decisions may have unforeseen impacts on users' privacy, especially if the algorithms operate in opaque ways. For example, AI-driven marketing tools might target vulnerable groups with exploitative ads, or facial recognition technologies may be misused to track individuals without their knowledge or consent.

- **Practical Advice**: Regularly assess AI-driven projects for potential privacy risks. Ensure that your data processing systems comply with data protection laws, such as the GDPR, and build in transparency by informing users how their data is being used.

2. How AI Can Introduce New Privacy Vulnerabilities

AI introduces several unique privacy risks not typically associated with traditional systems:

- **Data Aggregation**: AI systems often aggregate large amounts of data from multiple sources, which can create privacy vulnerabilities. By combining data from various touchpoints, AI can generate highly detailed user profiles, revealing sensitive aspects of a person's life.

- **Lack of Anonymization**: While AI systems may collect anonymous data at first, over time, the models may begin to re-identify individuals based on patterns in the data. This re-identification poses serious privacy risks.

- **Practical Advice**: Incorporate robust data anonymization and pseudonymization techniques during the AI model training phase to mitigate privacy vulnerabilities. Anonymization helps to reduce the risk of individuals being identified through aggregated data.

3. Case Studies of Privacy Issues Caused by AI Systems

Several incidents highlight how AI systems can cause privacy issues:

- **Cambridge Analytica Scandal**: In 2018, it was revealed that the data analytics company Cambridge Analytica harvested the personal data of millions of Facebook users without consent. The data was then used to target users with political ads, influencing elections. This case highlights how AI-driven data analysis can be misused to infringe on privacy, manipulate users, and violate consent.

  - **Impact**: This led to significant privacy violations, legal action, and a public outcry, forcing companies like Facebook to reassess their data practices and transparency efforts.

  - **Website**: Cambridge Analytica Scandal

- **Clearview AI Facial Recognition Technology**: Clearview AI developed a facial recognition system that scraped publicly available photos from social media sites without users' consent. This AI system posed a significant privacy risk as it allowed law enforcement agencies to identify individuals without their knowledge or consent.

  - **Impact**: Clearview AI faced lawsuits for violating privacy laws, and it raised ethical questions about consent and surveillance in AI-driven technologies.

  - **Website**: Clearview AI Controversy

Action Point

Assess privacy risks in your AI projects by identifying potential vulnerabilities such as data misuse, unintended consequences, and lack of proper safeguards. Regularly audit AI models to ensure that privacy risks are mitigated and that data processing practices remain transparent and ethical.

Checklist for DPOs to Address Privacy Risks in AI

- **Data Consent**: Ensure that all personal data used in AI projects has been obtained with proper consent.

- **Risk Assessment**: Regularly conduct privacy impact assessments (PIAs) to identify and mitigate privacy risks.

- **Anonymization**: Implement anonymization techniques where possible to protect user identities.

- **Transparency**: Clearly inform users about the data being collected and how it will be used.

- **Security Protocols**: Ensure AI systems are equipped with strong security measures to prevent breaches.

MOTD

"Privacy is the foundation of trust—build AI systems that respect both."

Chapter 3: AI and Data Privacy: A New Frontier
3.3 The Challenges of Balancing Innovation and Privacy

1. Striking a Balance Between Innovation and Regulatory Compliance

The rapid pace of AI development often leads to challenges in adhering to existing privacy regulations. Innovation and regulatory compliance can sometimes seem at odds:

- **Innovation Pressure**: AI systems can unlock new opportunities, from personalized services to predictive analytics, but pushing forward with innovation often involves processing large amounts of personal data. This can run afoul of data protection laws like the GDPR if proper safeguards aren't in place.

- **Regulatory Compliance**: Regulations like GDPR impose strict guidelines on how data can be collected, processed, and used. While these regulations aim to protect user privacy, they can be seen as a barrier to the swift development and deployment of AI systems.

- **Practical Advice**: To strike a balance, organizations should integrate privacy by design. This involves embedding privacy protections into AI systems from the start, ensuring both regulatory compliance and room for innovation. Privacy Impact Assessments (PIAs) should be a routine part of AI projects, especially when new data sources or methods are involved.

2. Managing Stakeholder Expectations

Stakeholders—ranging from investors to customers—often have different expectations when it comes to AI systems:

- **Investor Expectations**: Investors may prioritize rapid growth and breakthrough innovations, sometimes pushing for aggressive data collection strategies to fuel AI models.

- **Customer Concerns**: On the other hand, customers are increasingly aware of their privacy rights. They expect organizations to handle their data responsibly, with transparency and care.

- **Practical Advice**: DPOs can play a key role in managing these conflicting interests by facilitating clear communication between stakeholders. By educating stakeholders on the importance of privacy and how it can be integrated into innovation, DPOs help create a shared understanding of the value of both privacy and innovation.

3. Evaluating the Trade-offs Between Data Utility and Privacy

There are always trade-offs between the utility of data and the privacy of individuals. Organizations must evaluate these trade-offs carefully:

- **Data Utility**: AI thrives on large datasets to make predictions and create personalized experiences. However, the more data collected, the greater the risk of infringing on individuals' privacy.

- **Privacy Protection**: Collecting less data or anonymizing it can reduce privacy risks, but this might limit the AI model's effectiveness or capabilities.

- **Practical Advice**: Data minimization strategies, such as only collecting necessary data and anonymizing sensitive data, can help balance these two needs. Additionally, offering users more control over their data, such as giving them the ability to opt-in or opt-out of specific data collection methods, fosters trust.

4. Real-World Examples of Balancing Innovation and Privacy

- **Example 1: Apple's Privacy Features in iOS**
  Apple has been a leader in promoting privacy while maintaining innovation. With features like App Tracking Transparency and Privacy Labels on the App Store, Apple has set a standard for balancing the demand for personalization (innovation) with a commitment to user privacy.

  - **Impact**: This approach has helped Apple gain user trust, positioning it as a privacy-conscious brand. At the same time, it encourages developers to be more transparent about data usage.

  - **Website**: Apple's Privacy Features

- **Example 2: Google's AI in Healthcare (DeepMind)**
  Google's DeepMind AI system has made significant strides in healthcare, particularly with its AI algorithms for diagnosing diseases. However, the company faced significant challenges regarding privacy when it used patient data from the UK's National Health Service (NHS) for training purposes without adequate consent.

  - **Impact**: This sparked public backlash, raising awareness about how organizations handle sensitive medical data. In response, Google took steps to address privacy concerns by updating its privacy policies and ensuring more transparency.

  - **Website**: DeepMind Health

Action Point

To ensure both innovation and privacy, create a framework within your organization that integrates privacy into the AI development process. Regularly assess the potential privacy risks, engage with stakeholders to align expectations, and implement data minimization strategies to protect user data.

Checklist for Balancing Innovation and Privacy in AI

- **Privacy by Design**: Ensure that privacy considerations are embedded into AI development from the start.

- **Data Minimization**: Collect only the data necessary for the AI system to function.

- **Transparency**: Be clear with users about how their data is used and give them control over it.

- **Stakeholder Communication**: Regularly communicate with stakeholders about privacy challenges and how they are being addressed.

- **Regulatory Monitoring**: Stay updated on privacy regulations to ensure compliance with laws like GDPR.

MOTD

"Balancing innovation and privacy are not a compromise—it's a partnership for a responsible digital future."

Chapter 3: AI and Data Privacy: A New Frontier
3.4 The Role of Data Minimization in AI

1. The Importance of Minimizing Data Collection in AI Systems

In the AI landscape, **data minimization** is a critical principle for safeguarding privacy and ensuring compliance with regulations like the GDPR. Minimizing data collection reduces the risk of breaches and the potential for misuse:

- **Reducing Exposure**: The less personal data collected, the lower the risk of exposure in the event of a data breach. Collecting only the necessary data ensures that organizations aren't storing unnecessary information that could potentially harm users if compromised.

- **Regulatory Compliance**: GDPR and similar laws emphasize the importance of collecting only the **minimum** necessary data for a specific purpose. Organizations that adhere to this principle not only comply with the law but also demonstrate a commitment to user privacy, which can build trust.

- **Practical Advice**: Establish clear guidelines within your organization about what data is essential for AI models and avoid the temptation to gather excessive data "just in case." AI models can often work well with less data if it's well-curated and targeted.

2. Techniques for Data Anonymization and Aggregation

Data anonymization and aggregation are key techniques that help reduce the risk of personal data exposure while maintaining the usefulness of data:

- **Anonymization**: This involves removing any identifiable information from data, making it impossible to trace back to any individual. For example, removing names, addresses, and other identifiers from datasets allows companies to process the data without violating privacy.

- **Aggregation**: Aggregating data means combining individual data points into broader groups or categories, such as age ranges or geographical regions, so that personal details are not exposed. This approach is often used in predictive analytics, where individual data points are not necessary for generating valuable insights.

- **Practical Advice**: AI developers should implement robust anonymization techniques, such as **k-anonymity** (where data cannot be re-identified within a group of at least 'k' individuals) and **differential privacy** (adding noise to data to prevent individual identification). Both techniques make data safer for processing while still maintaining its utility for AI models.

3. Best Practices for Reducing Data Exposure in AI Algorithms

To ensure that AI systems minimize the exposure of sensitive data, several best practices can be followed:

- **Data Encryption**: Encrypt sensitive data both in transit and at rest to prevent unauthorized access.

- **Access Control**: Limit access to personal data to only those who absolutely need it to perform their job functions. Role-based access control (RBAC) can help achieve this.

- **Regular Audits**: Perform regular audits and reviews of AI systems to assess whether any unnecessary data is being collected or exposed.

- **Practical Advice**: Regularly monitor and audit AI systems to ensure compliance with privacy standards. Create a strong internal policy around data minimization that includes training staff and AI developers about best practices in data protection.

4. Real-World Examples of Data Minimization in AI

- **Example 1: Apple's Use of Differential Privacy**
  Apple has integrated **differential privacy** into its systems, particularly in iOS, to collect user data for improving services while preserving privacy. For instance, when collecting usage data from users to improve the predictive text feature, Apple adds "noise" to the data to prevent individual identification, ensuring that the data remains anonymized while still providing valuable insights.

  - **Impact**: This approach allows Apple to improve its AI systems without sacrificing user privacy. It demonstrates how large-scale data can be processed for innovation while minimizing privacy risks.

  - **Website**: Apple's Differential Privacy

- **Example 2: Google's Federated Learning**
  Google uses **Federated Learning**, a technique that allows AI models to be trained across many decentralized devices while keeping the data on-device rather than transferring it to central servers. This approach minimizes the exposure of personal data by ensuring that sensitive data never leaves the device.

  - **Impact**: Federated learning enables Google to use large-scale data to improve its AI models (such as for predictive typing or photo recognition) without compromising user privacy. It significantly reduces the risk of data breaches and complies with privacy standards.

  - **Website**: Google Federated Learning

Action Point

Implement data minimization techniques in your AI design process. Regularly audit your data practices and ensure that only the data necessary for AI models is collected. Use techniques like anonymization, aggregation, and differential privacy to protect user data and maintain compliance with privacy regulations.

Checklist for Data Minimization in AI

- **Collect only necessary data**: Avoid collecting excess data that may not be required for the AI model's purpose.

- **Use anonymization and aggregation**: Implement robust methods to anonymize and aggregate data before use.

- **Ensure encryption**: Encrypt sensitive data to prevent unauthorized access.

- **Limit access**: Restrict data access to only those who need it.

- **Audit AI systems regularly**: Conduct audits to check for any unnecessary data collection or privacy risks.

MOTD

"Data minimization is not just a legal requirement, it's a responsible approach to creating safer, more trusted AI systems."

Chapter 3: AI and Data Privacy: A New Frontier
3.5 The Role of the DPO in AI Privacy Management

1. Monitoring AI Technologies for Compliance with Privacy Standards

The **Data Protection Officer (DPO)** plays a crucial role in ensuring that AI technologies comply with privacy standards and regulations like GDPR. This responsibility involves:

- **Ongoing Compliance Checks**: The DPO needs to regularly monitor AI systems to ensure that data handling practices align with privacy laws. This includes checking how personal data is collected, processed, and stored by AI systems.

- **Ensuring Purpose Limitation**: AI systems must only process personal data for the purposes it was originally collected for. The DPO must ensure that data is not repurposed without proper consent.

Practical Advice: Implement automated compliance checks within AI systems to flag potential violations. Regularly update your compliance protocols to reflect evolving privacy laws, ensuring AI systems are consistently in line with privacy regulations.

2. Auditing AI Systems and Reporting Findings to Leadership

Auditing AI systems is a key function for the DPO to ensure that AI technologies adhere to internal privacy policies and external regulations. This includes:

- **Conducting Data Protection Impact Assessments (DPIAs)**: These assessments evaluate how AI systems impact privacy and data protection. DPIAs should be conducted regularly, especially when implementing new AI models or processing new types of data.

- **Reporting to Leadership**: The DPO must communicate audit findings to top management, ensuring that leadership is aware of privacy risks and compliance gaps. This ensures that AI projects remain aligned with the organization's overall data protection strategy.

Practical Advice: Develop a clear reporting structure and dashboard for tracking AI system audits. Highlight key privacy risks, potential breaches, and necessary actions for leadership review.

3. Ensuring Transparency and User Control Over Personal Data

AI systems can often feel like "black boxes" where decisions are made without clear explanations. The DPO ensures that:

- **Transparency**: AI systems must be designed in a way that makes it clear to users how their data is being used. This could include detailed privacy policies, accessible explanations of how AI makes decisions, and user notifications when data is collected or processed.

- **User Control**: It is vital to provide users with control over their personal data. For example, giving users the option to opt-in or opt-out of data collection, or providing them with easy access to update or delete their personal information.

Practical Advice: Implement user-friendly tools that allow individuals to easily manage their data preferences. Also, ensure that AI systems provide explanations when users interact with the technology, particularly in sensitive areas such as credit scoring or healthcare.

4. Real-World Examples of DPOs in AI Privacy Management

- **Example 1: IBM Watson's AI and Data Privacy**
  IBM's Watson has been used across various industries, including healthcare, to provide AI-driven insights. As part of their data privacy strategy, IBM ensures that data used for training Watson's AI systems is anonymized and only processed for the intended purpose. The DPO plays an active role in conducting audits and ensuring that all data usage adheres to privacy regulations like HIPAA.

  - **Impact**: IBM's commitment to compliance and privacy has fostered trust in Watson's AI, particularly in sensitive fields like healthcare.

  - **Website**: IBM Watson AI and Data Privacy

- **Example 2: The European Commission's AI Audits**
  The European Commission has implemented regular audits of AI systems deployed across EU institutions, ensuring compliance with the **General Data Protection Regulation (GDPR)**. The DPO of the EU oversees these audits, ensuring transparency and data protection. Audits are conducted for AI systems processing personal data, and findings are reported to EU leadership to ensure compliance with European privacy standards.

  - **Impact**: These audits increase public confidence in AI technologies used by governmental bodies, ensuring they meet the stringent privacy standards set by the GDPR.

  - **Website**: European Commission AI Strategy

5. Action Point

As a DPO, be proactive in embedding privacy considerations into the AI system design and development process. Regularly audit AI systems, track compliance, and ensure transparency and user control. Share the audit findings with leadership to ensure data privacy is always a priority.

Checklist for DPOs in AI Privacy Management

- **Monitor AI for compliance**: Regularly assess AI technologies for compliance with privacy laws and organizational standards.

- **Conduct DPIAs**: Perform data protection impact assessments for new AI projects and technologies.

- **Ensure transparency**: Implement clear communication on how AI processes personal data.

- **Provide user control**: Enable users to access, update, or delete their personal data as necessary.

- **Report findings to leadership**: Regularly communicate audit findings and privacy risks to senior management.

MOTD

"Privacy isn't just about compliance—it's about building trust. Every step you take toward protecting user data makes AI better for everyone."

Chapter 4: The Ethical Dimensions of AI

4.1 Defining AI Ethics

1. What is AI Ethics and Why It Matters

AI ethics refers to the study and application of ethical principles in the design, development, and deployment of AI technologies. It is concerned with ensuring that AI systems operate in ways that are morally sound and just, respecting human rights, and minimizing harm. As AI increasingly influences everyday decisions—ranging from job hiring processes to credit scoring—ethics becomes essential to ensure that AI systems are not only effective but also fair and responsible.

AI ethics matters because unchecked AI development can lead to consequences such as discrimination, biases, invasions of privacy, and loss of human agency. These challenges arise when AI systems, which are designed to make decisions based on data, inadvertently perpetuate societal biases or undermine ethical principles such as fairness, equality, and transparency.

Practical Advice: Always ask, "What could go wrong?" when developing AI. Recognize potential ethical dilemmas from the start to integrate safeguards, like bias detection or transparency mechanisms, into your design.

2. The Principles of Fairness, Accountability, and Transparency

Three core principles that guide AI ethics are **fairness**, **accountability**, and **transparency**. These principles help ensure that AI systems are not only technically sound but ethically responsible.

- **Fairness**: AI systems should treat all individuals and groups impartially. This includes addressing algorithmic bias that could disadvantage certain groups based on race, gender, or socioeconomic status.

- **Accountability**: Developers must be accountable for the decisions made by AI systems. If an AI system harms an individual or a community, those responsible for its design and deployment should face consequences.

- **Transparency**: AI systems should be explainable, meaning their decision-making processes should be understandable to humans. Users should have insight into how and why decisions are made, especially in sensitive areas like healthcare or criminal justice.

Practical Advice: Use tools like **fairness toolkits** and **audit trails** to make AI systems more accountable. Regularly test for biases and ensure that AI systems are transparent by using explainable AI (XAI) methods.

3. Key Ethical Frameworks for AI Development

Several ethical frameworks help guide AI development, ensuring that it aligns with societal values:

- **The IEEE Global Initiative on Ethics of Autonomous and Intelligent Systems**: This initiative provides guidelines for designing AI systems that respect human rights, ensure fairness, and avoid bias. It emphasizes inclusivity and the consideration of diverse perspectives.

- **The EU Ethics Guidelines for Trustworthy AI**: Developed by the European Commission's High-Level Expert Group on AI, these guidelines focus on ensuring AI systems are lawful, ethical, and robust. The guidelines include provisions for privacy protection, accountability, and the transparency of AI systems.

By following these frameworks, organizations can make ethical AI development an integral part of their processes, ensuring alignment with global standards and societal expectations.

Practical Advice: Familiarize yourself with **Ethical AI frameworks** and apply them in your work. Adopting these frameworks early on can reduce the risks of AI misuse and help build user trust.

4. Real-World Examples of AI Ethics in Action

- **Example 1: Google's AI Principles**
  Google's **AI principles** outline their commitment to ensuring AI is used ethically. They focus on fairness, privacy, transparency, and accountability. For example, Google's AI principles specifically emphasize the prevention of discriminatory or biased outcomes, particularly in critical areas like health, law enforcement, and education.

  - **Impact**: By adhering to these ethical principles, Google aims to build AI technologies that benefit all people while minimizing harm, particularly in vulnerable communities.

  - **Website**: Google AI Principles

- **Example 2: The Facial Recognition Ban by San Francisco**
  In 2019, San Francisco became the first major U.S. city to ban the use of **facial recognition technology** by city agencies. This decision was based on ethical concerns over privacy, bias, and the potential for mass surveillance. The city felt that AI technologies, if used without proper ethical oversight, could harm civil liberties and disproportionately affect minority communities.

  - **Impact**: This ban helped protect the rights of citizens by preventing the uncontrolled spread of AI technologies that might have violated privacy or fairness principles.

  - **Website**: San Francisco Facial Recognition Ban

5. Action Point

To apply AI ethics in your work, familiarize yourself with common AI ethics guidelines and frameworks. Incorporate principles of fairness, accountability, and transparency into AI system design, and keep track of the ethical implications of AI as technology evolves.

Checklist for AI Ethics in Development

- **Fairness**: Regularly test AI systems for biases and ensure equitable outcomes.

- **Accountability**: Define roles and responsibilities for those developing and deploying AI systems.

- **Transparency**: Make AI decision-making processes explainable to users and stakeholders.

- **Ethical Frameworks**: Adopt guidelines like IEEE and EU Trustworthy AI to guide AI development.

MOTD

"Ethical AI isn't just about following rules—it's about shaping a future where technology serves humanity with fairness, transparency, and accountability."

Chapter 4: The Ethical Dimensions of AI
4.2 Potential Ethical Issues in AI Deployment

1. Bias and Discrimination in AI Algorithms

AI systems learn from vast amounts of data, but if that data is biased, the AI can replicate and even amplify those biases. For example, an AI used in hiring might be trained on historical data, which could reflect past hiring decisions that were influenced by gender or racial biases. This results in a system that may unintentionally discriminate against certain groups, even if the algorithm itself is designed to be impartial.

Practical Advice: Ensure the data used to train AI models is diverse and representative. Regularly audit AI systems for bias by using fairness detection tools like IBM's AI Fairness 360. Consider alternative data sets that are balanced and not skewed toward any particular demographic group.

2. Unintended Societal Impacts of AI Technologies

AI deployment often has far-reaching consequences beyond the immediate goals it was designed for. For instance, AI-powered surveillance systems can improve public safety but could also infringe on privacy rights. Similarly, automated decision-making systems in criminal justice or lending could unintentionally affect vulnerable communities if they aren't properly calibrated to avoid reinforcing systemic inequalities.

Practical Advice: Think beyond the primary use case of the AI technology. Identify possible long-term consequences, such as impacts on social equity, job displacement, or individual freedoms. Work with ethicists, sociologists, and community groups to evaluate the wider implications.

3. The Risks of AI Systems That Lack Transparency

Many AI algorithms, especially deep learning models, are often seen as "black boxes," meaning they make decisions without providing a clear rationale for those decisions. This lack of transparency can lead to issues like accountability, where it's difficult to pinpoint the cause of an error or justify decisions to the affected parties. It also fosters a lack of trust in the technology, especially in sensitive areas like healthcare or criminal justice.

Practical Advice: Use explainable AI (XAI) techniques to increase transparency. Consider frameworks like the **LIME (Local Interpretable Model-agnostic Explanations)** or **SHAP (Shapley Additive Explanations)** to provide understandable insights into how AI models make decisions. This ensures that stakeholders understand AI outcomes and feel confident in the system's integrity.

4. Action Point

Identify potential ethical risks early in your AI projects. Conduct regular audits of the AI models you deploy and stay updated on ethical guidelines. Engage with diverse teams to ensure that all perspectives are considered in the AI design and decision-making process.

Real-World Examples

- **Example 1: Amazon's AI Hiring Tool** Amazon developed an AI system to assist in hiring decisions but found that it was biased against women. The AI was trained on resumes submitted to Amazon over a 10-year period, which were predominantly from male candidates, leading to an algorithm that penalized resumes with words associated with women (e.g., "women's" or "female"). This case highlights how bias can be unintentionally coded into AI systems.

    - **Impact**: The issue was discovered, and Amazon discontinued the tool. This example demonstrates the importance of auditing AI systems to avoid biased outputs.

    - **Website**: Amazon's AI Hiring Tool

- **Example 2: COMPAS Algorithm in Criminal Justice** The COMPAS algorithm is used in the U.S. to assess the likelihood of a criminal reoffending. However, investigations revealed that the algorithm was biased against African Americans, predicting a higher risk of reoffending compared to white defendants with similar criminal histories. This case demonstrates how the lack of transparency in AI models can lead to significant ethical and societal consequences.

    - **Impact**: The use of COMPAS raised ethical questions about fairness, accountability, and transparency in AI-driven criminal justice decisions.

    - **Website**: ProPublica's Analysis of COMPAS

Checklist for Identifying and Addressing Ethical Risks in AI

- **Bias and Discrimination**: Test for and address potential biases in data and models.

- **Transparency**: Use tools and methods to make AI systems interpretable and explainable.

- **Unintended Consequences**: Consider societal impacts beyond the immediate scope of the AI system.

- **Continuous Monitoring**: Regularly audit AI systems post-deployment for ethical compliance.

MOTD

"Ethical AI is not about creating perfect systems, but about making responsible choices that protect people and society."

Chapter 4: The Ethical Dimensions of AI
4.3 Why Ethics Should Be a Priority in AI Design

1. The Long-Term Consequences of Unethical AI Systems

AI systems have the potential to influence society on a grand scale, shaping decisions that impact people's lives. If AI systems are designed without careful consideration of ethical implications, the consequences can be far-reaching. For example, unethical AI in the financial sector can lead to biased lending practices, exacerbating inequality. In healthcare, AI-driven diagnostic tools that lack ethical oversight could result in misdiagnosis, particularly for underrepresented groups.

Practical Advice: Start with ethical considerations from day one. Incorporate ethical review panels in the design phase to ensure that the system's potential impact is fully understood. This involves both technical teams and stakeholders from social sciences or ethics backgrounds to assess long-term consequences.

2. Case Studies of AI Ethics Gone Wrong

Many AI systems have caused harm due to a lack of ethical considerations in their design. A famous example is the **Tay chatbot**, developed by Microsoft in 2016. The chatbot, designed to engage with users on Twitter, quickly became notorious for repeating offensive and inflammatory statements after learning from user interactions. This mishap illustrates how AI systems, when poorly controlled or ethically unchecked, can unintentionally harm brands and individuals.

Practical Advice: Conduct stress tests on AI systems by simulating real-world scenarios before deployment. These tests should look for unintended consequences, such as harmful biases, offensive language, or discrimination, and help to identify weak points in the design.

3. Ethical AI as a Competitive Advantage

AI ethics is not just a regulatory obligation; it is a competitive advantage. Ethical AI fosters trust among users and customers, building strong reputations. Companies that prioritize ethics in AI design can differentiate themselves in a crowded marketplace, particularly in industries where trust is paramount, such as healthcare, finance, and education. Companies that fail to prioritize ethics risk backlash, lawsuits, or loss of customer confidence.

Practical Advice: Position your company as an industry leader in responsible AI by being transparent about the ethical standards followed during development. Certifications or collaborations with ethical AI organizations can also boost credibility. Companies like **Google** have adopted frameworks for AI ethics and have been transparent about their approach to addressing bias and fairness.

4. Action Point

Prioritize ethical AI design from the very beginning. Integrate ethics reviews and diverse stakeholder input into the AI development lifecycle. This proactive approach will help to mitigate risks, ensure fairness, and build trust with users.

Real-World Examples

- **Example 1: The Failure of Microsoft's Tay AI** In 2016, Microsoft launched Tay, an AI chatbot designed to interact with Twitter users. Unfortunately, within hours, Tay began to tweet racist and offensive comments, as it was influenced by the offensive inputs from users. The lack of ethical boundaries in Tay's learning process highlighted the need for responsible AI design and real-time oversight.

  - **Impact**: Microsoft had to shut down Tay and apologize publicly, demonstrating how lack of ethical foresight can result in reputational damage and loss of trust.

  - **Website**: Microsoft Tay

- **Example 2: IBM's Watson for Oncology** IBM's Watson for Oncology was designed to assist doctors by suggesting cancer treatment plans based on medical records and clinical trials. However, Watson's recommendations were not always aligned with real-world medical practice. In some instances, Watson suggested unsafe or incorrect treatment plans due to a lack of sufficient data validation and ethical checks in its decision-making processes.

  - **Impact**: The failure to consider all ethical and practical factors in AI's medical deployment raised concerns about patient safety. It highlighted the importance of ensuring that AI systems, especially those used in high-stakes environments like healthcare, are designed with thorough ethical safeguards.

  - **Website**: IBM Watson Health

Checklist for Prioritizing Ethics in AI Design

- **Early Ethical Review**: Involve ethicists, legal experts, and diverse teams from the design phase.

- **Bias Audits**: Regularly test for and mitigate biases in data and algorithms.

- **Transparency**: Ensure transparency in how decisions are made by the AI system.

- **Stakeholder Engagement**: Involve affected parties (e.g., customers, employees) to understand their concerns and address them.

- **Continuous Monitoring**: Post-deployment, continuously monitor AI systems to ensure ethical standards are upheld.

MOTD

"Building ethical AI isn't just about avoiding mistakes; it's about creating systems that enhance trust and societal good."

Chapter 4: The Ethical Dimensions of AI
4.4 The DPO's Role in AI Ethics Implementation

1. Ensuring AI Systems Follow Ethical Guidelines

The Data Protection Officer (DPO) is not only responsible for compliance with data privacy laws but also plays a critical role in ensuring that AI systems adhere to ethical guidelines. This means working closely with AI developers and product teams to integrate ethical considerations into the AI development process, such as fairness, transparency, accountability, and the avoidance of bias. The DPO can ensure that AI systems do not breach these ethical principles by reviewing their design, functionality, and the data they are trained on.

Practical Advice: The DPO should actively participate in AI system development from the outset. Ensure ethical guidelines are in place before AI models are deployed. Regularly review both the AI system's design and its real-world consequences. This could involve setting up a "pre-launch audit" or "ethical impact assessment" to ensure that all ethical issues are identified and addressed before launch.

2. Monitoring AI Decision-Making for Ethical Alignment

AI systems are often designed to make autonomous decisions based on algorithms and data inputs. The DPO's role is to monitor these decisions to ensure they align with ethical standards. This could involve tracking how AI systems make decisions, assessing the fairness of these decisions, and ensuring transparency in decision-making processes. The DPO should ensure that users or stakeholders can understand why an AI system made a particular decision, particularly in sensitive areas such as hiring, lending, or healthcare.

Practical Advice: To monitor AI decision-making, the DPO should regularly audit AI systems for biases and ensure the decisions made by AI systems are transparent and explainable. Implement tools that allow tracking and recording decision-making processes, which can be reviewed if there are concerns about discrimination or unfair outcomes.

3. How the DPO Serves as an Advocate for Ethical AI

As an advocate for ethical AI, the DPO must ensure that the organization maintains a strong ethical stance on AI use. This means advocating for transparent practices, pushing for the elimination of biases, and ensuring the fair and equitable treatment of all individuals impacted by AI systems. The DPO also acts as the bridge between AI developers, company leadership, and regulatory authorities, ensuring that ethical considerations are prioritized and communicated effectively across all stakeholders.

Practical Advice: The DPO should act as a proactive voice in AI ethics discussions. Regularly provide input on AI development processes, ensure transparency in AI models, and promote ethical training within the organization. This helps foster a culture of ethical awareness and responsibility among all employees involved in AI development.

4. Action Point

Establish clear procedures to enforce ethical standards in AI. These procedures should involve setting up ethics committees, implementing regular AI audits, developing decision-making transparency protocols, and ensuring there are processes to handle complaints or issues related to ethical concerns in AI.

Real-World Examples

- **Example 1: The Role of DPO in IBM Watson Health** IBM Watson Health's AI-powered solutions have been applied to various industries, including healthcare, to assist in decision-making. The DPO played a vital role in ensuring that these AI systems adhered to strict ethical guidelines, including privacy regulations and unbiased decision-making. For instance, in deploying AI for medical diagnosis, the DPO ensured that patient data was anonymized, and AI decisions were based on clear and transparent guidelines.

  - **Impact**: By maintaining a robust ethical framework, IBM ensured that Watson Health's AI-powered systems were trustworthy and compliant with regulations. This allowed healthcare professionals to use AI confidently, knowing the ethical and legal implications were well-managed.

  - **Website**: IBM Watson Health

- **Example 2: The DPO's Role in AI Transparency at Google** Google, in response to concerns around AI ethics, implemented a framework to address potential biases and transparency issues in its AI systems. The DPO at Google ensured that these frameworks were regularly updated and adhered to, helping monitor the AI algorithms for any discriminatory practices and advocating for transparency in how data was being used. Google's DPO worked with both internal teams and external regulators to develop clearer guidelines on how AI should function fairly.

  - **Impact**: Google became a leader in advocating for ethical AI, with transparency reports and public policy documents showing their commitment to fairness, privacy, and ethics. The DPO's advocacy ensured AI systems were aligned with both ethical principles and regulatory requirements.

  - **Website**: Google AI Ethics

Checklist for Implementing Ethical AI Procedures

- **Ethics Reviews**: Implement mandatory ethics reviews at every stage of AI development.

- **Bias Audits**: Regular audits of AI systems to identify and mitigate any potential biases.

- **Transparency Protocols**: Establish clear documentation and procedures for ensuring decision-making transparency.

- **Stakeholder Engagement**: Involve diverse stakeholders in the design and monitoring of AI systems.

- **Compliance with Regulations**: Ensure that AI systems comply with all relevant data privacy and ethical guidelines.

- **Complaint Mechanism**: Set up an easy-to-use system for reporting concerns about AI-related ethical violations.

MOTD

"Ethical AI is not just about avoiding harm, it's about creating technology that benefits all."

Chapter 4: The Ethical Dimensions of AI
4.5 Addressing Ethical Dilemmas in AI

1. Navigating Complex Ethical Challenges in AI Design

Designing AI systems comes with inherent ethical challenges, especially when these systems influence important aspects of life, such as healthcare, employment, and financial decisions. Ethical dilemmas often arise around issues like algorithmic bias, transparency, fairness, and accountability. A Data Protection Officer (DPO) plays a crucial role in navigating these challenges by ensuring that AI systems align with ethical standards, protecting individuals' rights, and preventing potential harm.

Practical Advice: When navigating ethical dilemmas in AI design, the DPO should prioritize fairness and transparency, especially in areas that significantly impact people's lives. Collaboration with data scientists, ethicists, and legal teams is essential to identify potential ethical risks early in the design process. If an AI model might perpetuate bias or produce unfair outcomes, the DPO must advocate for redesign or additional safeguards to ensure ethical alignment.

2. Developing Decision-Making Frameworks for the DPO

The DPO needs a structured decision-making framework to address ethical dilemmas effectively. This framework should include clear guidelines for assessing the ethical implications of AI systems, prioritizing data privacy, fairness, and transparency. It should also include processes for reviewing decisions made by AI systems, providing feedback, and making adjustments where necessary. Establishing this framework empowers the DPO to make informed decisions when facing ethical conflicts.

Practical Advice: Develop a decision-making flowchart or guidelines that outline the key ethical considerations and steps to take when confronted with an AI-related ethical dilemma. For example, assess whether the AI system has a potential for bias, whether user consent has been obtained, and whether data privacy is maintained. This step-by-step approach will provide consistency in ethical decision-making and improve transparency.

3. Balancing Business Goals with Ethical Principles

AI projects are often driven by business goals, such as increasing efficiency, maximizing profits, or gaining a competitive edge. However, these goals must be balanced with ethical principles. For the DPO, this means ensuring that business objectives do not overshadow the importance of privacy, fairness, or transparency. The DPO must help the business make ethical trade-offs, ensuring that AI solutions are not just profitable but also fair, accountable, and compliant with data protection laws.

Practical Advice: The DPO should guide business leaders on how ethical principles can align with business goals. This could involve highlighting the long-term benefits of ethical AI, such as improved customer trust and regulatory compliance. A solid ethical approach often leads to better customer retention, reduced risk of legal issues, and a competitive advantage in industries increasingly concerned with ethical technology.

4. Action Point: Create an Ethics Review Board for AI Projects in Your Organization

To address ethical dilemmas effectively, consider creating an ethics review board within your organization. This board would consist of multidisciplinary experts, including data privacy professionals, ethicists, legal advisors, and AI developers, to review AI projects and assess potential ethical risks before deployment. The board would also monitor the implementation of ethical standards and offer advice on handling ethical challenges.

Practical Advice: As a DPO, you can take the initiative to form an ethics review board that meets regularly to assess AI development projects. This board can provide an ongoing, cross-functional approach to ensuring AI systems are designed, deployed, and operated ethically. It can also serve as a sounding board for decision-making when ethical concerns arise.

Real-World Examples

- **Example 1: The Ethical Dilemma in Amazon's AI Hiring Tool** Amazon developed an AI-powered hiring tool intended to streamline recruitment. However, it was discovered that the system was biased against female candidates because it was trained on historical data that favored male candidates. The DPO and ethics committee were instrumental in halting the use of this tool and redesigning it to eliminate the bias. They introduced a new set of guidelines to ensure that future AI systems would undergo rigorous ethical reviews before being deployed.

  - **Impact**: This example shows how a proactive approach to ethics, involving continuous oversight and collaboration with AI teams, can prevent harmful biases from entering decision-making processes.

  - **Website**: Amazon AI Hiring Tool

- **Example 2: The Role of DPO in Facebook's AI Content Moderation** Facebook has faced several ethical dilemmas related to the use of AI in content moderation, particularly concerning privacy and free speech. The DPO played a key role in ensuring that AI systems used for content moderation were transparent and did not violate privacy regulations. Facebook implemented a review system where AI-generated decisions could be scrutinized, and users were notified about the moderation actions taken.

  - **Impact**: Facebook's approach highlighted the importance of balancing business goals (such as content moderation efficiency) with ethical concerns (such as transparency, privacy, and fairness). The DPO's role in advocating for ethical AI helped mitigate risks of discrimination and ensure that content moderation was fair.

- o **Website**: Facebook Content Moderation

Checklist for Ethical Decision-Making Framework in AI

- **Bias Mitigation**: Ensure AI models are regularly audited for bias.

- **Transparency**: Ensure AI systems are explainable, and decisions can be traced back to their origins.

- **Stakeholder Engagement**: Engage diverse stakeholders to ensure ethical concerns are addressed.

- **Compliance**: Align AI systems with legal, regulatory, and ethical standards.

- **Continuous Review**: Set up regular reviews of AI systems post-deployment to track their ethical performance.

MOTD

"Ethical AI isn't just about compliance; it's about building trust that lasts."

Chapter 5: Legal Frameworks and Regulations Affecting DPOs

5.1 The General Data Protection Regulation (GDPR)

1. Key Provisions of GDPR, DPDP Act 2023 (DPDPA) Affecting AI and Data Protection

The General Data Protection Regulation (GDPR) is a fundamental legal framework for data protection within the European Union (EU), establishing stringent requirements for organizations that process personal data. As AI systems heavily rely on personal data, GDPR's provisions, such as the right to data erasure (the "right to be forgotten"), data minimization, and the need for explicit consent, are particularly relevant. The **DPDP Act 2023 (DPDPA)**, India's answer to GDPR, echoes similar principles of data protection but also introduces new norms applicable to AI.

Practical Advice: For Data Protection Officers (DPOs), it's crucial to ensure AI systems are compliant with these regulations. This includes ensuring data is processed lawfully, transparency in data usage, and users' rights are respected, such as giving them control over their data. AI should only use personal data necessary for its function, and individuals must be informed of how their data is used in AI algorithms.

2. Rights of Individuals Under GDPR and DPDPA

Both GDPR and DPDPA give individuals several key rights over their personal data, which AI systems must respect:

- **Right to Access**: Individuals can request access to the data organizations hold on them.

- **Right to Rectification**: Individuals can request corrections of inaccurate data.

- **Right to Erasure**: The right to be forgotten allows individuals to request the deletion of their data.

- **Right to Restriction of Processing**: Individuals can limit the processing of their data under certain conditions.

Practical Advice: As a DPO, ensure AI systems are designed to provide individuals with these rights seamlessly. For example, if a user requests data deletion, AI systems must ensure that their data is fully erased without affecting the functionality of the AI model.

3. Fines and Penalties for Non-Compliance

Non-compliance with GDPR can lead to severe fines and penalties. For instance, companies can be fined up to **€20 million** or **4% of global annual turnover**, whichever is higher, for breaching data protection rules. The DPDPA follows a similar structure but introduces different thresholds for penalties and fines, especially in cases of severe violations such as data breaches involving sensitive data.

Practical Advice: DPOs should be proactive in ensuring AI systems comply with these regulations to avoid hefty fines. This involves conducting regular audits, implementing security measures, and ensuring that systems have sufficient safeguards to protect personal data. Organizations must also document compliance activities for regulatory inspections.

4. Action Point: Ensure Your AI Systems Comply with GDPR Guidelines

To ensure compliance, DPOs should regularly assess AI systems and implement the following:

- Conduct Data Protection Impact Assessments (DPIAs) to identify and mitigate privacy risks.
- Review AI models to ensure they adhere to principles like data minimization and accuracy.
- Ensure that the AI systems provide adequate user consent and transparency.
- Regularly train AI development teams on GDPR and DPDPA requirements.

Practical Advice: DPOs should work closely with AI developers and legal teams to ensure that all aspects of the AI lifecycle — from data collection to data processing — are compliant with the GDPR and DPDPA. This ensures a balanced approach between compliance and innovation.

Real-World Examples

- **Example 1: Google's GDPR Fine for Data Privacy Violations** In 2019, Google was fined €50 million by the French data protection regulator for breaching GDPR rules. The fine stemmed from Google's lack of transparency and inadequate consent mechanisms for personalized ads. Google failed to adequately inform users about how their data would be used and did not provide clear consent options.

    - **Impact**: This fine highlighted the importance of transparency and consent in data processing. It emphasized that AI-driven systems, especially those using personal data for advertising, must ensure clear user consent and transparency in line with GDPR.

    - **Website**: Google GDPR Fine

- **Example 2: India's DPDPA Compliance by IT Companies** With the introduction of the **Data Protection Bill 2023 (DPDPA)** in India, several IT companies such as Infosys and Tata Consultancy Services (TCS) have started evaluating their compliance structures to align with both global GDPR norms and local DPDPA regulations. These companies are enhancing their privacy policies and AI practices to ensure that AI models adhere to the new data protection laws in India.

- **Impact**: These companies are investing in AI data governance frameworks to avoid penalties and safeguard user rights. This proactive approach not only ensures compliance but also improves consumer trust and confidence in AI-driven services.

- **Website**: India's Data Protection Bill

Checklist for GDPR & DPDPA Compliance in AI Systems

- **Conduct DPIAs**: Regularly assess potential privacy risks in AI projects.

- **Transparency**: Ensure AI systems are transparent in their data usage.

- **User Consent**: Implement clear and explicit consent mechanisms.

- **Data Minimization**: Collect only the data necessary for AI functionalities.

- **Rights Management**: Ensure mechanisms for data access, rectification, and erasure are in place.

- **Regular Audits**: Perform regular audits to ensure ongoing compliance.

MOTD

"Compliance is not just about avoiding penalties; it's about building trust and protecting individuals' rights."

Chapter 5: Legal Frameworks and Regulations Affecting DPOs
5.2 Other Key Regulations and Their Impact on AI

1. The California Consumer Privacy Act (CCPA)

The **California Consumer Privacy Act (CCPA)**, enacted in 2020, is a landmark privacy regulation in the U.S., focused on protecting consumer data privacy rights in California. CCPA grants individuals the right to know what personal data is being collected, the right to request deletion of data, and the right to opt out of the sale of their data. For AI systems, this means that any company using AI that processes personal data of California residents must comply with CCPA's requirements.

Practical Advice: DPOs should ensure AI systems that process California residents' data provide transparency in data collection and offer mechanisms for opting out of data sales. It is also crucial for AI systems to include a clear process for data deletion requests and to limit the amount of personal data collected to what is necessary for AI functionalities.

2. The EU Artificial Intelligence Act (AI Act)

The **EU Artificial Intelligence Act**, proposed in 2021, is the first comprehensive regulatory framework aimed at governing AI usage across the European Union. The Act categorizes AI systems into different risk levels, from minimal to high risk, and establishes requirements for each category. High-risk AI systems, such as those used in critical infrastructures, biometric identification, and legal processes, are subject to stricter requirements, including transparency, human oversight, and risk assessment procedures.

Practical Advice: DPOs working with AI technologies in the EU must be aware of these classifications and implement relevant compliance measures. High-risk AI systems will need to undergo rigorous impact assessments, and organizations must ensure human oversight, fairness, and transparency in AI decision-making processes.

3. Other Global Frameworks and Emerging Regulations

Around the world, there is growing interest in regulating AI to ensure ethical use, transparency, and fairness. Some notable examples include:

- **China's AI Guidelines**: China introduced guidelines in 2021 to enhance AI governance, focusing on ethical principles, data protection, and social impact. AI companies in China must ensure their systems are transparent, accurate, and do not infringe on public interests.

- **Brazil's General Data Privacy Law (LGPD)**: Similar to the EU's GDPR, the LGPD imposes strict data protection regulations on businesses operating in Brazil, with requirements around data consent, portability, and breach notifications, affecting how AI models process personal data.

Practical Advice: DPOs need to monitor global regulatory trends and ensure that their organization's AI systems comply with local laws, which can vary greatly across regions. For international companies, this may mean developing a flexible compliance framework that accommodates multiple legal landscapes.

4. Action Point: Stay Informed on the Global Regulatory Landscape for AI and Data Protection

Given the dynamic nature of AI regulation, staying informed on evolving global frameworks is crucial. DPOs should engage in continuous monitoring of legal developments and adapt their data protection practices accordingly.

Practical Steps:

- Subscribe to newsletters and regulatory updates on data privacy and AI laws.

- Regularly review AI models and data processing practices to ensure alignment with the latest legal requirements.

- Engage in forums, webinars, and industry groups to stay ahead of emerging trends.

Real-World Examples

1. **Example 1: Salesforce and the CCPA** Salesforce, a leading customer relationship management (CRM) platform, was quick to comply with CCPA by updating its data collection processes and providing users with easy-to-navigate tools for managing their data preferences. Salesforce made it possible for users to request the deletion of personal information, opt out of data sales, and understand how their data was being used, thus enhancing customer trust.

- **Impact**: By adopting CCPA-compliant measures, Salesforce avoided potential legal issues and built customer loyalty through transparency.

- **Website**: Salesforce and CCPA Compliance

2. **Example 2: DeepMind and the EU AI Act** In response to the EU's forthcoming **AI Act**, DeepMind, an AI research company, has been working to ensure that its AI systems meet the regulatory requirements for transparency and fairness. DeepMind's systems, which use AI for healthcare applications, are being audited for ethical and legal compliance to meet the EU's standards for high-risk AI systems.

- **Impact**: By proactively aligning with the EU AI Act's provisions, DeepMind avoids future regulatory hurdles and ensures its AI systems contribute positively to healthcare while maintaining ethical standards.

- **Website**: DeepMind and AI Ethics

Checklist for DPOs to Stay Updated on Global Regulations

- **Regular Legal Reviews**: Schedule periodic legal reviews to ensure compliance with the latest regulations in key jurisdictions.

- **Develop Flexible Policies**: Create policies that allow for easy updates based on new regulatory developments.

- **Collaborate with Legal Teams**: Work closely with legal teams to interpret the impact of new laws on AI practices.

- **Training**: Provide continuous training for AI developers and legal teams on emerging regulations and compliance strategies.

MOTD

"Staying ahead of regulation isn't just about avoiding penalties; it's about shaping AI innovation responsibly and ethically."

Chapter 5: Legal Frameworks and Regulations Affecting DPOs
5.3 Compliance Strategies for DPOs in AI Development

1. Developing a Compliance Checklist for AI Systems

A robust compliance checklist is essential for ensuring that AI systems meet regulatory requirements and ethical standards. The checklist should cover key areas such as data privacy, consent mechanisms, algorithm transparency, and compliance with specific laws like GDPR, CCPA, and the EU AI Act.

Practical Advice:

- **Data Collection**: Ensure data is collected in a lawful, transparent, and fair manner.

- **Data Minimization**: Limit data to what is necessary for AI model functionality.

- **Data Subject Rights**: Verify that AI systems respect user rights, including access, rectification, and deletion of personal data.

- **Accountability**: Establish clear responsibilities for AI data processing and decisions.

The checklist can be used to guide the development process, ensuring compliance is embedded from the start.

2. Conducting Regular Audits and Assessments

DPOs must implement regular audits to evaluate how AI systems adhere to privacy regulations and ethical guidelines. These audits should focus on both technical aspects, such as data security, and operational aspects, such as algorithmic fairness and transparency.

Practical Advice:

- **Risk Assessments**: Regularly conduct Data Protection Impact Assessments (DPIAs) for AI systems, especially high-risk applications.

- **Security Audits**: Audit AI systems for data breaches, unauthorized access, and other security vulnerabilities.

- **Algorithm Audits**: Regularly evaluate AI models for biases, transparency issues, and discriminatory outcomes.

Regular audits ensure that any issues or non-compliance are identified early and addressed before they escalate into significant risks.

3. Collaboration Between Legal, Technical, and Ethical Teams

AI systems must meet the complex intersection of legal, technical, and ethical requirements. DPOs should facilitate collaboration between these teams to ensure

AI systems are developed and maintained in compliance with regulations and ethical standards.

Practical Advice:

- **Legal Team**: Ensure that legal experts are involved in drafting and reviewing privacy policies, user agreements, and AI deployment strategies.

- **Technical Team**: Work closely with engineers to design AI systems with privacy by design and data protection measures in mind.

- **Ethical Team**: Engage ethicists or AI ethics boards to assess the fairness, accountability, and transparency of AI systems.

Cross-functional collaboration helps align AI development with compliance standards and fosters an environment of responsible AI innovation.

4. Action Point: Implement a Robust AI Compliance Program Within Your Organization

A comprehensive AI compliance program should be an ongoing, dynamic process that integrates AI ethics, data protection, and legal frameworks into every stage of AI development. DPOs need to ensure that their organization has the right structures, policies, and tools in place to monitor and maintain compliance.

Practical Steps:

- **Create an AI Compliance Team**: Designate roles responsible for overseeing AI compliance and ethical considerations within the organization.

- **Training and Awareness**: Regularly train staff on the latest AI regulations, data protection laws, and ethical AI practices.

- **Use Compliance Tools**: Implement tools that assist with tracking AI compliance, including audit logs and automated reporting systems.

Real-World Examples

1. **Example 1: IBM Watson and GDPR Compliance** IBM Watson Health, an AI-driven healthcare platform, faced significant regulatory challenges around data privacy. By creating a comprehensive compliance program that incorporated GDPR requirements, IBM ensured that its AI models used in healthcare adhere to data protection standards, including clear consent mechanisms and secure data handling practices.

   - **Impact**: This proactive approach allowed IBM to avoid hefty fines and safeguard patient data, ensuring Watson's AI technology could be used in the European Union.

   - **Website**: IBM Watson and GDPR

2. **Example 2: Google and AI Audits** Google has developed an internal system of regular AI audits, which include algorithmic fairness assessments, security evaluations, and privacy checks. These audits help ensure that AI products like Google Assistant and Google Ads comply with legal requirements and ethical standards. The company also collaborates with external experts to provide third-party verification.

   - **Impact**: This comprehensive auditing process not only helps Google avoid legal penalties but also builds trust among users by demonstrating a commitment to ethical AI.

   - **Website**: Google AI Ethics

Checklist for DPOs in AI Compliance

Action Item	Details
Compliance Checklist Creation	Develop a checklist covering data privacy, transparency, and ethical guidelines for AI.
Conduct Regular Audits	Schedule regular audits for risk assessments, data protection, and ethical considerations.
Cross-functional Collaboration	Establish communication channels between legal, technical, and ethical teams to ensure compliance.
Implement Training Programs	Conduct training for developers, data scientists, and staff on AI regulations and privacy laws.
Track AI Compliance	Use automated tools to monitor and track compliance in real-time.

MOTD

"AI development is a marathon, not a sprint; compliance is the foundation of responsible innovation."

Chapter 5: Legal Frameworks and Regulations Affecting DPOs
5.4 Data Subject Rights and AI

1. The Rights of Individuals in the AI-Driven Data Landscape

In the context of AI, data subject rights refer to the entitlements granted to individuals regarding their personal data. Under laws like the GDPR, individuals have the right to access, correct, delete, and object to the processing of their personal data. These rights ensure that individuals can maintain control over their data, even when it is used in AI-driven systems.

Practical Advice:

- **Right to Access**: Individuals must be able to request and obtain copies of their personal data processed by AI systems.

- **Right to Rectification**: If AI systems store inaccurate or outdated data, individuals have the right to request corrections.

- **Right to Erasure (Right to be Forgotten)**: Individuals can request the deletion of their data if it is no longer necessary or if they withdraw consent.

- **Right to Object**: Individuals have the right to object to automated decision-making and profiling based solely on AI algorithms, especially in sensitive areas like credit scoring or hiring.

2. How AI Systems Should Respect Data Subject Rights

AI systems need to be designed with privacy and data subject rights in mind. This involves implementing features that allow for transparency, consent management, and user control over personal data. AI systems should also provide mechanisms to comply with individuals' requests for access, correction, or deletion of their data.

Practical Advice:

- **Transparency**: Inform users about how their data is being used, especially when AI algorithms are involved.

- **Data Portability**: Allow individuals to request and receive their data in a structured, commonly used format to move it to another service.

- **Consent Management**: Implement easy-to-use mechanisms to obtain, withdraw, and track consent for AI systems that process personal data.

3. Managing Access Requests and Data Corrections in AI Systems

Handling access requests and data corrections within AI systems can be complex due to the volume and dynamic nature of data processed. However, ensuring compliance with data subject rights is crucial. Systems should be able to identify, retrieve, and allow changes to personal data, even if it's embedded within large datasets or used by machine learning models.

Practical Advice:

- **Data Retrieval**: Implement features in AI systems that allow for easy identification and retrieval of personal data, even if it's part of an AI model's learning process.

- **Correction Processes**: Ensure that there are clear processes for users to request corrections and that these corrections are propagated across all instances of the data used by AI models.

- **Audit Trails**: Maintain an audit trail of data subject requests to demonstrate compliance with legal requirements.

4. Action Point: Ensure AI Systems Respect Data Subject Rights Under the Law

To ensure AI systems comply with data subject rights, DPOs should embed privacy protections into AI development from the start. This can be achieved by integrating privacy by design principles and continuously monitoring AI systems to make sure they respect the rights of individuals.

Practical Steps:

- **Privacy by Design**: Develop AI systems with built-in mechanisms to uphold data subject rights.

- **Regular Monitoring**: Continuously monitor AI systems for compliance with data subject rights.

- **Training**: Ensure staff are well-trained in handling data subject rights requests related to AI systems.

Real-World Examples

1. **Example 1: Facebook's Data Access Requests**
   In response to regulatory scrutiny, Facebook (now Meta) has developed processes for individuals to access and manage their personal data within its platform. Users can see what data Facebook's AI systems use to target advertisements and can request changes or deletions, aligning with data subject rights under GDPR.

   - **Impact**: By allowing users to manage their data, Meta mitigates privacy concerns and complies with GDPR while building user trust.

   - **Website**: Facebook Data Access

2. **Example 2: Apple's "Privacy" Feature**
   Apple's commitment to user privacy includes a feature that allows individuals to review and manage the data collected by its AI systems. Users can see the

data Apple uses for Siri, Maps, and other AI-driven services, and they can control the types of data shared or request its deletion.

- o **Impact**: By offering transparency and control over personal data, Apple demonstrates a proactive approach to respecting data subject rights, which enhances user confidence in its products.

- o **Website**: Apple Privacy

Checklist for Ensuring AI Systems Respect Data Subject Rights

Action Item	Details
Transparency Mechanisms	Implement clear information on how AI processes personal data and provides rights.
Access Requests	Ensure AI systems can retrieve personal data when requested.
Correction and Deletion Mechanisms	Establish clear processes to allow individuals to correct or delete their data.
Consent Management	Provide easy-to-use tools to allow users to manage and withdraw consent.
Audit Trails	Maintain records of data subject requests for compliance auditing.

MOTD

"Data subject rights are the backbone of ethical AI; prioritize them for a future where privacy and innovation coexist."

Chapter 5: Legal Frameworks and Regulations Affecting DPOs
5.5 The Role of the DPO in Legal Compliance

1. How DPOs Ensure Compliance with Data Protection Laws in AI Systems

Data Protection Officers (DPOs) play a critical role in ensuring AI systems comply with relevant data protection laws such as the GDPR, DPDPA, and other global regulations. Compliance in AI systems requires DPOs to monitor how personal data is collected, processed, stored, and used by AI technologies.

Practical Advice:

- **Data Audits**: DPOs should conduct regular audits of AI systems to ensure that they comply with data protection principles like data minimization, purpose limitation, and data accuracy.

- **Impact Assessments**: Under GDPR, DPOs are required to perform Data Protection Impact Assessments (DPIAs) for AI systems that process sensitive data or engage in automated decision-making.

- **Compliance Checklists**: Develop compliance checklists to ensure that AI systems incorporate the necessary data protection measures from design to deployment.

2. The DPO's Role in Facilitating Communication Between Stakeholders

As a bridge between stakeholders, DPOs ensure that all parties—such as legal teams, AI developers, and regulatory bodies—are aligned with data protection requirements. Effective communication between stakeholders is vital for ensuring that AI systems are developed and deployed in accordance with legal standards.

Practical Advice:

- **Liaison with Legal Teams**: The DPO should work closely with legal experts to interpret data protection laws and ensure they are appropriately applied to AI systems.

- **Collaboration with AI Developers**: Regular discussions with AI development teams help the DPO understand how personal data is used and ensure privacy and security measures are integrated from the design phase.

- **Stakeholder Education**: Educating stakeholders about the importance of data protection in AI ensures everyone understands their roles in maintaining compliance.

3. Preventative Strategies to Mitigate Legal Risks

DPOs are responsible for anticipating potential legal risks in AI systems and implementing preventive measures. These strategies reduce the likelihood of data breaches, non-compliance penalties, and other legal issues related to AI technologies.

Practical Advice:

- **Privacy by Design**: Implement privacy by design and default principles to minimize risks. This involves embedding data protection into the AI system's architecture and development lifecycle.

- **Regular Legal Training**: Ensure that the organization's employees are trained in legal compliance, particularly those involved in AI development or handling personal data.

- **Risk Assessment**: DPOs should proactively assess legal risks related to new AI technologies and ensure that mitigation strategies (such as encryption or pseudonymization) are in place.

4. Action Point: Be a Proactive Leader in Legal Compliance for AI Systems

DPOs must take a proactive approach to compliance by anticipating changes in the legal landscape and continuously monitoring the AI system for adherence to regulatory requirements. This proactive stance is essential for maintaining the organization's legal standing and protecting individuals' privacy.

Practical Steps:

- **Stay Updated on Regulations**: DPOs must stay informed about evolving data protection laws and emerging AI-related regulations. Subscribe to relevant legal updates and participate in industry events.

- **Establish Clear Reporting Mechanisms**: Create clear reporting mechanisms so that stakeholders can report any data privacy concerns related to AI systems promptly.

- **AI Compliance Program**: Develop a formal AI compliance program within the organization that ensures all AI systems undergo regular legal assessments and audits.

Real-World Examples

1. **Example 1: IBM's AI Fairness 360 Toolkit**
   IBM has developed the AI Fairness 360 toolkit, which is designed to help organizations identify and mitigate bias in AI algorithms. This tool helps companies comply with regulations such as the GDPR by ensuring that AI models are transparent and fair, avoiding discriminatory practices that could result in legal risks.

   - **Impact**: IBM's initiative helps businesses align AI systems with fairness principles, reducing the risk of legal challenges and penalties related to biased AI outcomes.

- Website: AI Fairness 360 Toolkit

2. **Example 2: Microsoft's AI Ethics Guidelines**

   Microsoft has established AI ethics guidelines that help its teams navigate legal and ethical challenges in AI development. The company's commitment to AI ethics, including transparency and accountability, is a direct response to regulatory requirements and has helped it avoid legal pitfalls.

   - **Impact**: Microsoft's proactive approach ensures legal compliance while maintaining user trust and avoiding potential legal issues related to AI misuse.

   - **Website**: Microsoft AI Ethics

Checklist for DPOs to Ensure Legal Compliance in AI Systems

Action Item	Details
Data Protection Impact Assessment (DPIA)	Conduct DPIAs for AI systems, especially those involving sensitive data.
Compliance Audits	Perform regular audits of AI systems to ensure adherence to data protection laws.
Privacy by Design	Ensure privacy measures are integrated into the AI system's architecture.
Stakeholder Collaboration	Foster communication between legal, technical, and AI teams for compliance.
Legal Training	Provide ongoing training on legal compliance and data protection for relevant teams.

MOTD

"Stay ahead of legal challenges by integrating compliance into the DNA of your AI systems from day one."

Chapter 6: Risk Management in AI and Data Protection

6.1 Identifying and Assessing AI Risks

1. Types of Risks in AI Projects

AI systems can present various types of risks that could impact data privacy, security, fairness, and operational efficiency. Understanding these risks is crucial for developing strategies to mitigate them. Here are the primary risk categories:

- **Privacy Risks**: AI systems often handle vast amounts of personal data, making them prone to breaches or misuse. Data privacy risks include unauthorized access to sensitive data, non-compliance with privacy laws (e.g., GDPR), and improper data sharing.

- **Security Risks**: AI systems can be vulnerable to cyberattacks like adversarial attacks, data poisoning, and model inversion, where hackers manipulate input data to influence outcomes or access confidential information.

- **Bias Risks**: AI systems are susceptible to inheriting biases from the data they are trained on. This can result in unfair, discriminatory, or unrepresentative outcomes, particularly in sensitive applications like hiring or lending decisions.

- **Operational Risks**: These include the potential for AI models to malfunction or perform sub optimally due to poor data quality, inadequate training, or lack of monitoring, which can lead to financial losses or operational inefficiencies.

2. Risk Assessment Techniques for AI Projects

Effective risk management in AI requires the use of specialized techniques to identify, evaluate, and address potential risks. Some common techniques include:

- **Threat Modeling**: A systematic approach to identify potential security threats, privacy vulnerabilities, and operational risks in AI systems. This helps determine how different components of the system may be exposed to attacks or breaches.

- **Scenario Analysis**: This technique involves considering different "what-if" scenarios to assess how AI systems might fail or behave unexpectedly under various conditions, such as data breaches or model bias.

- **Root Cause Analysis (RCA)**: RCA is used to understand the underlying causes of AI failures, allowing organizations to prevent future issues and ensure AI systems perform as expected.

3. Frameworks for Evaluating AI Risks

Several frameworks have been developed to assess and manage risks in AI projects. These frameworks typically combine principles of risk management with the unique challenges posed by AI technologies. Some widely used frameworks include:

- **NIST AI Risk Management Framework**: The National Institute of Standards and Technology (NIST) provides a comprehensive framework that helps organizations assess, manage, and mitigate risks related to AI systems. The NIST framework covers areas such as data privacy, model transparency, and fairness.

- **ISO/IEC 27001**: This framework is focused on information security management but can be adapted to AI projects to ensure that data privacy and security risks are mitigated effectively.

4. Action Point: Develop a Comprehensive AI Risk Assessment Process

To effectively manage AI risks, organizations need a robust risk assessment process. DPOs and AI teams should collaborate to develop and implement a comprehensive risk assessment plan. The process should include:

- **Identifying potential risks** at every stage of the AI lifecycle, from data collection and model training to deployment and monitoring.

- **Evaluating the impact and likelihood** of each risk, considering both short-term and long-term consequences.

- **Implementing risk mitigation strategies** such as enhanced security protocols, data anonymization, and regular audits.

Real-World Examples

1. **Example 1: Amazon's AI Hiring Tool**
   Amazon developed an AI-powered recruitment tool that was later scrapped after it was discovered that the system was biased against female candidates. The algorithm was trained on resumes that were historically male dominated, leading to gender bias in hiring decisions.

   - **Impact**: This case highlights the operational and ethical risks of deploying AI systems without proper bias testing. The system led to discriminatory hiring practices, which could have resulted in legal and reputational consequences.

   - **Website**: Amazon's AI Hiring Tool

2. **Example 2: Uber's Self-Driving Car Accident**
   In 2018, an Uber self-driving car struck and killed a pedestrian in Arizona. An investigation revealed that the AI system had failed to detect the pedestrian in time, raising concerns about the reliability and safety of autonomous vehicles.

- o **Impact**: This incident underscores the operational and security risks of AI systems, especially those deployed in high-risk scenarios like autonomous vehicles. It led to further regulatory scrutiny on AI technologies in public safety contexts.
- o **Website**: Uber Self-Driving Car Incident

AI Risk Assessment Checklist

Action Item	Details
Risk Identification	Identify potential risks in privacy, security, bias, and operations.
Data Privacy Impact Assessment (DPIA)	Conduct DPIAs to evaluate privacy risks in AI systems.
Threat Modeling	Use threat modelling to assess AI system vulnerabilities.
Bias and Fairness Evaluation	Assess and mitigate any biases in AI algorithms using fairness audits.
Continuous Monitoring	Set up continuous monitoring of AI systems for potential failures.

MOTD

"Risk management in AI is not just about identifying dangers but about building smarter, safer, and more responsible systems from the start."

Chapter 6: Risk Management in AI and Data Protection
6.2 Developing Risk Mitigation Strategies

1. Building a Risk Mitigation Plan for AI Systems

To effectively manage AI-related risks, it's crucial to develop a structured risk mitigation plan. The process involves identifying potential risks, evaluating their impact, and creating strategies to minimize or eliminate these risks. The key steps in developing a risk mitigation plan include:

- **Risk Identification**: Pinpoint the specific risks associated with AI systems, such as data privacy concerns, security threats, operational failures, and biases.

- **Risk Assessment**: Evaluate the likelihood and impact of each risk, considering both short-term and long-term consequences.

- **Mitigation Strategies**: Implement controls such as stronger encryption, transparent algorithms, regular audits, and continuous model monitoring to mitigate identified risks.

2. Practical Tools and Techniques for Mitigating AI-Related Risks

Effective risk mitigation requires using specialized tools and techniques designed to address the unique challenges posed by AI systems:

- **Bias Audits**: Regularly audit AI algorithms to detect and eliminate biases. Tools like **IBM AI Fairness 360** and **Google's What-If Tool** are designed to assess fairness and identify discriminatory patterns in AI systems.

- **Explainability Tools**: To address the risk of lack of transparency, implement explainability tools such as **LIME (Local Interpretable Model-agnostic Explanations)** and **SHAP (Shapley Additive Explanations)**. These tools help clarify AI decision-making processes, making it easier to understand how models arrive at conclusions.

- **Penetration Testing**: Use cybersecurity tools like **OWASP ZAP** and **Burp Suite** to identify and address vulnerabilities in AI systems, ensuring they are resistant to attacks and breaches.

3. Integrating Risk Management into AI Project Lifecycles

Risk management should be embedded into every phase of the AI lifecycle. This ensures that risks are continuously monitored and mitigated from development through deployment and ongoing operations. Here's how risk management can be integrated:

- **Design Phase**: Implement privacy-by-design and security-by-design principles from the outset, considering risk factors such as data collection, model selection, and algorithm transparency.

- **Development Phase**: Regularly perform risk assessments and audits to ensure that any new code, features, or data sets do not introduce new vulnerabilities or biases.

- **Deployment Phase**: Continuously monitor AI systems for performance, security breaches, and compliance with data protection regulations (e.g., GDPR).

- **Post-Deployment**: Establish a feedback loop to evaluate AI performance and update models based on new data, user feedback, or identified risks.

4. Action Point: Create and Implement Risk Management Strategies for AI Systems

To mitigate AI risks effectively, organizations must be proactive. Develop a comprehensive risk management plan tailored to the AI system and ensure that it is regularly updated as the technology evolves. Collaborate with key stakeholders—technical teams, legal departments, and data protection officers (DPOs)—to ensure alignment on risk mitigation priorities.

Real-World Examples

1. **Example 1: Google's AI and Fairness Audits**
   Google has faced criticism over biased AI algorithms, especially regarding facial recognition systems. To mitigate these risks, Google adopted regular **AI fairness audits** using tools like the **AI Principles** and **What-If Tool**, which identify potential biases during the model development and testing phases. The company has since improved its AI systems' fairness by addressing gender and racial biases in facial recognition.

   - **Impact**: By implementing these audits, Google has improved the inclusivity of its AI systems, reducing reputational and legal risks associated with biased algorithms.

   - **Website**: Google AI Fairness

2. **Example 2: Microsoft's Risk Mitigation in AI-powered Hiring Systems**
   Microsoft's AI-powered hiring tools faced backlash when reports revealed biases against women and underrepresented minorities in hiring decisions. In response, Microsoft worked to develop and deploy more inclusive hiring AI systems by incorporating **bias detection algorithms** and revising training data to ensure diversity.

   - **Impact**: By embedding fairness checks and balancing the training data, Microsoft not only mitigated legal risks but also improved the transparency and equity of their hiring processes.

   - **Website**: Microsoft AI Ethics

Risk Mitigation Strategy Checklist

Action Item	Details
Risk Identification	Identify privacy, security, operational, and bias risks in AI systems.
Bias Detection and Mitigation	Implement tools to audit and reduce biases in AI models (e.g., IBM Fairness 360).
Transparency and Explainability	Use explainability tools to enhance model transparency (e.g., LIME, SHAP).
Security Testing	Conduct penetration testing to identify vulnerabilities.
Continuous Monitoring	Monitor AI systems for performance, security, and compliance post-deployment.

MOTD

"Building resilience in AI systems starts with proactive risk management—ensure that your systems not only innovate but do so responsibly."

Chapter 6: Risk Management in AI and Data Protection
6.3 Tools and Techniques for Managing AI Risks

1. Risk Monitoring and Control Techniques

To manage AI risks effectively, organizations need to establish robust risk monitoring and control techniques. These techniques are designed to track, identify, and mitigate risks throughout the AI system lifecycle. Key techniques include:

- **Real-Time Monitoring**: Continuously track AI models in real-time to detect issues such as model drift (i.e., when the model's performance deteriorates over time), security vulnerabilities, or data breaches. Tools like **Prometheus** and **Grafana** allow for real-time system health monitoring and visual dashboards.

- **Incident Management**: Develop incident response protocols for AI-related risks, including the rapid identification of vulnerabilities or failures, ensuring timely corrective actions. Techniques like **root cause analysis** help identify underlying issues after incidents occur.

- **Manual and Automated Audits**: Conduct periodic audits to ensure compliance with data protection standards (e.g., GDPR) and internal risk management policies. AI models should undergo audits for fairness, security, and compliance with applicable regulations.

2. Automation Tools for Continuous Risk Evaluation in AI

Automation is key in managing AI risks at scale. Leveraging AI-driven tools for continuous evaluation helps organizations stay ahead of emerging threats and ensure the stability and compliance of their AI systems. Some valuable automation tools include:

- **AI Risk Management Platforms**: Platforms like **DataRobot** and **H2O.ai** provide AI risk evaluation capabilities that integrate automated risk assessments, model validation, and bias detection.

- **Automated Monitoring**: Tools like **Seldon** and **Fiddler AI** enable automated monitoring of model performance, identify potential biases, and assess the impact of new data inputs on model predictions.

- **Continuous Integration/Continuous Deployment (CI/CD)**: Integrating AI risk assessments into the CI/CD pipeline allows teams to automatically test AI systems as new data or features are introduced, ensuring that changes don't inadvertently increase risks.

3. Key Performance Indicators (KPIs) for AI Risk Management

To measure the effectiveness of AI risk management efforts, it's essential to define and monitor key performance indicators (KPIs). These KPIs help assess whether the

AI systems are meeting the desired risk management objectives. Common KPIs for AI risk management include:

- **Bias Detection Rate**: Percentage of bias-related issues detected and corrected during audits.

- **Model Accuracy & Drift Rate**: Measures of how well models continue to perform over time and how often their predictive accuracy declines.

- **Incident Response Time**: Average time taken to respond to and mitigate an identified risk or breach in the AI system.

- **Compliance Score**: Percentage of AI systems that comply with data protection laws (e.g., GDPR) after periodic audits.

4. Action Point: Invest in Tools for Ongoing AI Risk Management

To ensure ongoing risk management for AI systems, organizations should invest in tools that continuously evaluate risks and provide actionable insights. Selecting tools that focus on risk detection, bias mitigation, and performance monitoring is essential for long-term success. Implementing automated systems and using platforms that integrate seamlessly with existing AI infrastructures can improve efficiency and scalability.

Real-World Examples

1. **Example 1: Uber's AI Risk Management System**
   Uber developed an automated system for risk management that continuously monitors its AI-powered operations. For instance, Uber uses machine learning models to predict and mitigate fraud in its ride-hailing app. Automated fraud detection algorithms analyze patterns of behavior in real-time, identifying and blocking fraudulent activities before they impact users or drivers.

   - **Impact**: By integrating continuous monitoring, Uber ensures that its AI models remain effective and secure, minimizing operational disruptions and potential financial losses from fraud.

   - **Website**: Uber AI

2. **Example 2: H2O.ai's Automated Machine Learning Platform**
   H2O.ai's **Driverless AI** platform allows for automated model risk management by incorporating real-time performance monitoring and continuous model validation. The platform automatically detects changes in model accuracy and alerts teams to potential issues. It also integrates explainability tools to ensure the AI models align with organizational transparency and fairness standards.

   - **Impact**: The continuous risk monitoring provided by H2O.ai helps organizations in industries like finance and healthcare mitigate risks associated with model drift, bias, and non-compliance.

- Website: H2O.ai

Risk Management Tools Checklist

Tool/Technique	Purpose
Prometheus & Grafana	Real-time system health monitoring and visualization of AI risks.
Fiddler AI	Continuous monitoring and explainability tools for AI systems.
H2O.ai Driverless AI	Automated model performance monitoring, validation, and risk evaluation.
DataRobot	Automated AI risk assessment and model validation platform.
CI/CD Integration	Automate risk assessments in the development pipeline.

MOTD

"Risk management is not just a protective measure—it's an opportunity to build more resilient and trustworthy AI systems."

Chapter 6: Risk Management in AI and Data Protection
6.4 Crisis Management in AI Systems

1. Steps to Take in Case of an AI-Related Data Breach or Failure

In the event of a data breach or AI system failure, swift and structured action is essential to mitigate risks and restore trust. The steps involved are:

- **Immediate Containment**: The first priority is to contain the breach or failure. This involves isolating the affected systems to prevent further data leaks or operational disruptions. For instance, disabling AI models that are malfunctioning or causing harm can prevent widespread damage.

- **Incident Reporting**: After containment, notify relevant stakeholders, including internal teams (IT, legal, etc.) and external parties like regulatory authorities, as required by law. According to GDPR, data breaches must be reported to the relevant data protection authority within 72 hours.

- **Investigation and Analysis**: Conduct a thorough investigation to understand the root cause of the issue. In AI systems, failures could be due to data corruption, model drift, or external factors like cyberattacks. Using tools like **Seldon** or **Fiddler AI** can help track model performance and detect anomalies.

- **Recovery and Remediation**: Once the cause is identified, work on repairing and restoring the AI system. This might involve retraining models with clean data or implementing new safeguards to avoid similar failures in the future.

2. Responding to Public Concerns and Regulatory Scrutiny

Public concern and regulatory scrutiny are common following an AI-related crisis. Transparency and proactive communication are key to maintaining trust:

- **Public Communication**: Craft clear, concise messages that outline the situation, the steps being taken to address the issue, and how it will be prevented in the future. It's crucial to avoid legal jargon and focus on transparency. Companies like **Facebook** (Meta) and **Uber** have dealt with AI-related incidents by publicly acknowledging the issue and explaining the corrective actions being taken.

- **Regulatory Compliance**: Ensure that all actions comply with applicable regulations, such as GDPR, which mandates strict requirements for data breach handling. DPOs should lead the compliance efforts, ensuring that all stakeholders (internal and external) are informed, and that the organization is in line with legal obligations.

3. The Role of the DPO in Managing AI-Related Crises

The **Data Protection Officer (DPO)** plays a central role in managing AI-related crises. Key responsibilities include:

- **Leading the Response**: The DPO should take the lead in managing the crisis response, coordinating with legal, technical, and public relations teams. They are responsible for ensuring that privacy laws and regulations are adhered to during the crisis.

- **Communication with Authorities**: The DPO is often the point of contact for data protection authorities during a breach. Their role includes filing necessary reports, answering inquiries, and ensuring transparency throughout the process.

- **Post-Crisis Analysis**: After the crisis, the DPO should lead the post-mortem analysis, ensuring that all lessons are learned and that improvements are made in policies, technology, and risk management frameworks.

4. Action Point: Prepare a Crisis Management Plan for AI Risks

To be prepared for AI-related crises, organizations should develop and implement a comprehensive crisis management plan. This plan should:

- Include clear steps for identifying, containing, and reporting breaches or failures.

- Designate roles and responsibilities, particularly for the DPO, IT, legal, and communications teams.

- Provide templates for communicating with stakeholders, including customers, regulators, and the public.

- Regularly test and update the plan through simulations and tabletop exercises.

Real-World Examples

1. **Example 1: Facebook's (Meta) AI-driven Data Breach Incident**
   In 2018, Facebook faced a crisis when it was revealed that millions of users' personal data were mishandled by third-party apps due to flaws in its AI-driven data-sharing processes. Meta took swift action by implementing stronger data access controls, publicly acknowledging the breach, and updating its AI algorithms to enhance privacy protection.

   - **Impact**: The company faced significant regulatory fines (over $5 billion from the FTC) and reputational damage. However, their transparent communication helped regain some public trust.

   - **Website**: Meta Transparency

2. **Example 2: Uber's AI-Related Data Breach in 2016**
   Uber experienced a massive data breach in 2016, where hackers stole data related to 57 million drivers and passengers. The breach was covered up for a year, which resulted in significant reputational and financial consequences when it was revealed. Uber's response included compensating affected users and revamping its internal data protection practices.

   o **Impact**: The breach resulted in $148 million in settlement costs, legal scrutiny, and a decrease in user trust. Uber has since worked to improve its AI and data protection systems.

   o **Website**: Uber Breach Details

Crisis Management Checklist

Action Item	Details
Contain the Issue	Isolate affected systems to prevent further harm.
Incident Reporting	Notify internal stakeholders and regulatory bodies within required timelines.
Conduct Root Cause Analysis	Investigate the source of the breach/failure and document findings.
Public Communication	Issue clear, transparent statements about the situation.
Compliance Check	Ensure all actions align with regulatory requirements (e.g., GDPR).
Post-Crisis Analysis	Conduct a thorough review and implement preventive measures.

MOTD

"Preparation is the foundation of effective crisis management. Build your plans today, so you're ready for anything tomorrow."

Chapter 6: Risk Management in AI and Data Protection
6.5 The DPO's Role in Risk Management

1. How DPOs Monitor and Manage AI Risks on an Ongoing Basis

The role of the **Data Protection Officer (DPO)** extends beyond initial compliance checks to include ongoing monitoring of AI risks. To manage these risks effectively, DPOs should:

- **Continuous Risk Assessment**: DPOs must regularly review AI models to ensure they align with evolving legal, ethical, and regulatory frameworks. They need to evaluate AI performance, data usage, and security practices to identify potential risks. Automated tools, such as **AI Fairness 360** by IBM or **Fiddler AI**, can help monitor bias, fairness, and other AI-specific risks.

- **Real-Time Monitoring**: AI systems can drift over time, resulting in security vulnerabilities or compromised data privacy. The DPO needs to track AI performance continuously, using tools to detect unusual patterns or performance drops that might indicate data bias, incorrect outputs, or security breaches.

- **Collaboration with IT and Data Teams**: DPOs should work closely with IT departments to ensure that AI systems are continuously updated and patched to protect against vulnerabilities. This ensures both legal compliance and the ethical operation of AI technologies.

2. The DPO's Responsibility for Risk Communication within the Organization

The DPO must act as the communication bridge between technical teams, leadership, and external stakeholders. Responsibilities include:

- **Reporting to Leadership**: The DPO must provide regular risk management reports to leadership, detailing AI risks, compliance status, and mitigation strategies. These reports should help decision-makers understand the scope of AI-related risks and their potential business impact.

- **Internal Awareness**: DPOs are responsible for ensuring that all departments are aware of data protection and AI risks. This involves training internal teams on AI ethics, privacy laws, and security risks, helping them understand their roles in mitigating these issues.

- **Stakeholder Engagement**: In addition to internal communication, DPOs must be ready to communicate risks to external stakeholders, including customers and regulators, especially when data breaches or compliance violations occur.

3. Developing Risk Management Reports and Presenting Them to Leadership

To facilitate informed decision-making, DPOs need to develop comprehensive risk management reports. These reports should include:

- **Risk Identification**: A clear outline of identified AI risks (security, privacy, bias, etc.), with potential impacts on the organization.

- **Risk Mitigation Plans**: Detailed strategies to mitigate identified risks, along with timelines and resources required.

- **Compliance Updates**: A status update on how well AI systems comply with data protection laws, such as GDPR or CCPA.

These reports should be presented regularly (quarterly or biannually) to leadership to ensure alignment on risk management strategies. They also serve as a key tool in auditing AI systems for compliance and efficiency.

4. Action Point: Take Ownership of AI Risk Management within Your Organization

DPOs should take full responsibility for AI risk management by:

- Implementing regular assessments to identify risks.

- Creating and enforcing risk management plans.

- Collaborating with cross-functional teams to ensure risk mitigation strategies are followed.

- Ensuring AI systems stay aligned with ethical standards and legal requirements.

By proactively managing AI risks, the DPO not only ensures compliance but also helps safeguard the organization from financial and reputational damage.

Real-World Examples

1. **Example 1: Google's AI Risk Management Framework**
   Google has implemented a robust AI risk management framework, which includes continuous monitoring of AI systems to ensure they remain ethical, secure, and aligned with privacy laws. The company uses tools like **Google Cloud AI** to track and mitigate risks like bias and algorithmic fairness, ensuring compliance with both GDPR and internal ethical guidelines.

   - **Impact**: Google's framework helps it maintain public trust and avoid costly legal issues by addressing AI risks proactively.

   - **Website**: Google AI Ethics

2. **Example 2: Microsoft's AI Responsibility Framework**
   Microsoft has established a comprehensive AI risk management system that involves DPOs working closely with AI developers and IT teams to monitor and manage risks. They emphasize AI ethics, privacy, and security, integrating these values directly into the AI development lifecycle.

- o **Impact**: Microsoft has maintained a strong reputation for privacy and ethical AI, preventing regulatory fines and bolstering user confidence.
- o **Website**: Microsoft AI Ethics

Checklist for AI Risk Management Reporting

Item	Details
Risk Identification	List potential AI-related risks (e.g., privacy, security, bias).
Risk Assessment	Evaluate the impact and likelihood of each risk.
Mitigation Plan	Define strategies for addressing each risk identified.
Compliance Status	Provide updates on AI systems' alignment with legal requirements.
Reporting Schedule	Set regular intervals (quarterly/annually) for reporting.

FAQ

Q1: What is the primary responsibility of a DPO in AI risk management?
A1: A DPO is responsible for identifying and mitigating AI risks, ensuring compliance with privacy laws, and communicating these risks effectively within the organization and to external stakeholders.

Q2: How often should risk management reports be presented to leadership?
A2: Risk management reports should be presented regularly, typically on a quarterly or biannual basis, to ensure leadership is informed of ongoing risks and compliance statuses.

Q3: What tools can help monitor AI risks?
A3: Tools like **AI Fairness 360** by IBM and **Fiddler AI** can be used to monitor AI systems for bias, security vulnerabilities, and compliance with ethical guidelines, helping DPOs manage ongoing risks.

MOTD

"Ownership in risk management isn't just about compliance; it's about fostering trust and accountability in every AI system you manage."

Chapter 7: AI Transparency and Accountability

7.1 The Importance of Transparency in AI Systems

1. What Transparency in AI Means for Data Privacy

Transparency in AI refers to the clarity and openness with which AI systems operate, especially regarding the data they collect, process, and use. For **data privacy**, transparency is essential because:

- **Clear Data Usage**: Users must understand what data is collected, how it is used, and for what purposes. For instance, if AI is collecting personal information, the user should be explicitly informed, and their consent must be obtained.

- **User Control**: Transparency ensures that individuals have control over their data, including rights to access, modify, or delete their data. Transparent AI systems empower individuals with knowledge and control, aligning with data protection regulations like GDPR.

- **Minimizing Uncertainty**: With clear information, users are less likely to be uncertain or suspicious about how AI systems handle their data, reducing the risks of privacy violations.

2. The Ethical Need for AI Transparency in Data Usage

Ethically, transparency serves as the foundation for responsible AI usage. AI systems can have profound implications on individuals' privacy, security, and even human rights. Without transparency, AI systems may perpetuate biases or make decisions that users cannot question. Ethical AI transparency involves:

- **Explaining AI Decisions**: It's crucial for AI developers to make the decision-making process in AI systems explainable. If an AI system recommends loan approval or denial, users should be able to understand the factors influencing that decision.

- **Eliminating Bias**: Transparency helps identify and address biases in AI algorithms, as developers can clearly understand how decisions are made. Without transparency, unintended biases can remain hidden, harming marginalized groups.

3. How Transparency Builds Public Trust in AI Systems

For AI systems to be widely accepted, especially in sensitive areas like healthcare, finance, or law enforcement, they must be perceived as trustworthy. Transparency helps build that trust in several ways:

- **Accountability**: When AI systems are transparent, users can see how decisions are made, which increases accountability. Users are more likely to trust AI when they feel the system is accountable for its actions.

- **Regulatory Compliance**: Transparency shows that an AI system complies with laws and ethical standards, increasing trust with regulators and consumers alike.

4. Action Point: Advocate for Transparent AI Systems in Your Organization

To foster trust and meet legal obligations, DPOs should advocate for the integration of transparent practices in AI systems within their organizations. Key actions include:

- **Developing Clear Policies**: Establish and communicate transparent AI policies to both internal teams and external users.

- **Ensuring Explainability**: Ensure that AI systems are designed to be explainable and that end-users can easily access and understand how their data is used.

- **Transparency Audits**: Conduct regular audits of AI systems to assess their level of transparency and compliance with data privacy laws.

Real-World Examples

1. **Example 1: The European Union's GDPR and AI Transparency**
   Under the **General Data Protection Regulation (GDPR)**, transparency is a key requirement, especially for automated decision-making. GDPR mandates that individuals be informed when decisions are made solely by automated processes and gives them the right to contest such decisions. This regulation aims to create more transparency in AI systems used by companies in the EU.
   - **Impact**: It gives individuals more control over their data and builds trust between organizations and users.
   - **Website**: EU GDPR Portal

2. **Example 2: IBM's AI Fairness 360 Toolkit**
   IBM developed the **AI Fairness 360 Toolkit**, an open-source library to help developers understand and improve transparency in AI models. It provides a suite of algorithms to detect and mitigate bias, enabling developers to build AI models that are not only transparent but also fair.
   - **Impact**: This toolkit enhances transparency and accountability in AI, helping developers ensure that AI decisions are equitable and understandable.
   - **Website**: IBM AI Fairness 360

FAQ

Q1: Why is transparency important in AI systems?
A1: Transparency in AI systems ensures that data privacy is respected, builds public

trust, and provides clear insight into how AI decisions are made. It allows individuals to control their data and understand the AI processes affecting them.

Q2: How can organizations implement transparency in AI?
A2: Organizations can implement transparency by developing clear data usage policies, ensuring AI systems are explainable, and conducting regular transparency audits to ensure compliance with privacy regulations.

Q3: What are the legal consequences of not maintaining transparency in AI?
A3: Failing to maintain transparency in AI systems could lead to non-compliance with data protection laws such as GDPR, resulting in penalties, loss of customer trust, and reputational damage.

MOTD

"Transparency is the cornerstone of trust in AI — build it into your systems, and your users will build trust in you."

Chapter 7: AI Transparency and Accountability
7.2 Ensuring AI Systems Are Accountable

1. Who is Accountable When AI Systems Cause Harm?

When AI systems cause harm—whether it's a privacy violation, discrimination, or financial loss—the question of accountability becomes crucial. Accountability in AI systems can be complex, but ultimately, it falls to:

- **AI Developers**: Developers who create AI systems are responsible for ensuring that their algorithms and models are ethical, fair, and compliant with laws. They must take steps to prevent harm and build systems that align with transparency, fairness, and accountability principles.

- **Organizations Using AI**: Organizations that deploy AI systems are responsible for ensuring these systems are used ethically and do not cause harm to users or the public. This includes regularly monitoring AI outputs, evaluating risks, and complying with legal standards.

- **Third-party Vendors**: In cases where third-party vendors provide AI systems, these vendors can also be held accountable if their system causes harm due to flaws or biases in the system's design. Ensuring third-party accountability is crucial when adopting external AI solutions.

In practice, accountability should be shared across these parties, with clear roles and responsibilities defined in contracts, data-sharing agreements, and compliance frameworks.

2. Frameworks for Accountability in AI Design and Deployment

Accountability can be incorporated into AI design and deployment through various frameworks:

- **AI Ethics Guidelines**: Frameworks like the **EU AI Act** (proposed) and **OECD AI Principles** establish ethical guidelines for AI design and deployment. These frameworks emphasize the need for responsible AI use, outlining clear principles like fairness, transparency, and accountability.

- **Internal Governance**: Organizations can create internal policies or committees (e.g., AI ethics boards) to monitor and enforce accountability. These committees should review AI models, assess risks, and ensure that systems are compliant with legal and ethical standards.

- **Third-party Audits**: Independent audits by third parties can assess whether an AI system operates as intended and adheres to accountability standards. Regular audits are essential for ensuring that systems remain fair, transparent, and ethical over time.

3. The DPO's Role in Ensuring AI System Accountability

As the guardian of data privacy and compliance, the **Data Protection Officer (DPO)** plays a crucial role in ensuring AI system accountability by:

- **Monitoring AI Projects**: The DPO should oversee AI projects to ensure that personal data is handled in accordance with privacy laws and regulations. They should ensure that the AI system collects, processes, and stores data responsibly, avoiding any privacy violations.

- **Risk Management**: The DPO helps assess and mitigate risks associated with AI, such as data breaches, privacy violations, or unethical decisions. They must ensure the organization implements safeguards that limit AI-related harm.

- **Transparency and Reporting**: The DPO should push for transparency in AI systems and report any findings related to accountability. This includes advocating for explainable AI and clear communication of how AI decisions are made, which can be critical for public trust.

4. Action Point: Develop Accountability Standards for AI Within Your Organization

To ensure AI accountability within an organization:

- **Create Clear Accountability Policies**: Develop clear, actionable guidelines for AI system development, deployment, and monitoring. These should specify who is responsible for various aspects of AI, from data collection to system output.

- **Establish a Governance Framework**: Set up a governance body such as an AI ethics board to oversee the deployment and operation of AI systems. This group should consist of AI specialists, data scientists, legal experts, and ethics officers to ensure comprehensive oversight.

- **Conduct Regular Audits**: Implement periodic audits to assess the performance and accountability of AI systems, making necessary adjustments based on findings.

- **Train Stakeholders**: Ensure that employees, particularly those involved in AI development, understand the importance of accountability. Provide training on the ethical and legal implications of AI use.

Real-World Examples

1. **Example 1: Cambridge Analytica and Accountability**
   The **Cambridge Analytica** scandal highlighted a lack of accountability in AI systems, where personal data from millions of Facebook users were harvested without consent and used to influence political campaigns. The lack of transparency and accountability in how data was used led to global backlash and regulatory scrutiny.

- o **Impact**: The scandal led to stricter data privacy regulations like **GDPR** and increased demand for accountability in AI systems.

- o **Website**: Cambridge Analytica Scandal

2. **Example 2: Autonomous Vehicles and Accountability**
   In 2018, an **Uber self-driving car** struck and killed a pedestrian in Arizona. The incident raised questions about accountability in autonomous vehicle technology. Uber took responsibility for the incident, but the case sparked debates about the role of developers, manufacturers, and operators in ensuring the safety of AI-driven vehicles.

   - o **Impact**: The incident spurred regulatory changes around autonomous vehicles, emphasizing the need for accountability in AI deployment.

   - o **Website**: Uber Self-Driving Car Incident

FAQ

Q1: Who is held accountable if an AI system causes harm?
A1: Accountability can be shared between AI developers, the organization deploying the AI system, and third-party vendors. Each party must ensure the system is designed, deployed, and maintained ethically and legally.

Q2: What role does the DPO play in AI accountability?
A2: The DPO monitors AI systems to ensure compliance with data privacy laws, mitigates risks, and advocates for transparency and ethical decision-making in AI operations.

Q3: How can organizations ensure AI system accountability?
A3: Organizations can implement AI ethics frameworks, establish governance bodies, conduct regular audits, and ensure all stakeholders understand their accountability in developing and deploying AI systems.

MOTD

"Accountability in AI is not just about avoiding harm—it's about building systems that users can trust and depend on."

Chapter 7: AI Transparency and Accountability
7.3 Explaining AI Decisions to End-Users

1. The Right to Explanation Under Data Protection Laws

In many jurisdictions, such as under the **General Data Protection Regulation (GDPR)** in the European Union, individuals have the **right to explanation** when automated decisions significantly affect them. This right stems from the principle of transparency, ensuring that users are aware of how AI systems process their data and arrive at decisions.

- **GDPR Article 22** specifically protects individuals from solely automated decisions, including profiling, which have legal consequences. If AI systems are used to make decisions like credit scoring or hiring, organizations must ensure that users can request and receive an explanation of the decision-making process.

- **Implications for AI**: AI systems must be designed to provide clear, understandable reasons behind their actions. Organizations that deploy AI should ensure that users can easily exercise their right to explanation, especially when such decisions can impact their lives significantly, such as loan approvals or medical diagnoses.

2. Providing Understandable Explanations for AI Decisions

AI decision-making, particularly when based on complex machine learning models, can often seem like a "black box"—opaque and hard to understand for non-experts. However, to meet data protection laws and maintain trust, organizations must make these decisions understandable to end-users.

- **Simplify the Explanation**: Use plain language to explain how and why decisions are made. This includes detailing what data was used, the factors considered, and how these factors led to the final outcome.

- **Offer Interpretability**: Provide users with actionable insights on how to influence the outcome. For instance, if an AI model is used in recruitment, applicants could be given feedback on the areas they can improve to increase their chances.

- **Transparency Tools**: Some AI models, like decision trees or rule-based systems, are more explainable than others, such as deep learning models. But, even for complex models, tools like **LIME (Local Interpretable Model-agnostic Explanations)** or **SHAP (Shapley Additive Explanations)** can help in generating explanations that can be understood by the general public.

3. Best Practices for Communicating AI Logic and Outcomes to Users

- **Clear Communication Channels**: Organizations should proactively communicate to users when AI is being used in decision-making processes, especially in contexts like finance, healthcare, or hiring.

- **Proactive Disclosure**: Before users are impacted by AI decisions, they should be informed about how their data will be processed and what to expect from the decision-making system.

- **Provide Context**: In addition to the decision itself, users should understand the context in which AI operates. For example, in a medical setting, the user should know if the AI's role is advisory or if it directly influences the diagnosis.

- **Examples of Clear Explanation**: Amazon's **Alexa**, for instance, offers users an option to review and manage data privacy settings, making it easy to understand how their data is used to personalize experiences. This transparency helps build trust.

4. Action Point: Ensure That AI Decisions Are Explainable to End-Users

To ensure transparency and trust, organizations should:

- **Develop Explanation Mechanisms**: Integrate AI explanation capabilities directly into user interfaces. For example, if an AI system makes a decision, offer an option for the user to ask "Why?" and provide an understandable breakdown.

- **Ensure Accessibility**: Make sure that explanations are accessible for all users, including those with disabilities. This can be done through accessible design principles and multiple channels of communication.

- **Educate Users**: Train users on how AI works and the importance of transparency. A well-informed user base is more likely to trust the system and engage with it productively.

Real-World Examples

1. **Example 1: Credit Scoring in the UK** In the UK, the **FICO** score system, which is used by lenders to assess creditworthiness, has come under scrutiny for lack of transparency. To address this, FICO has started offering users more transparency regarding how their scores are calculated and how they can improve them.

    - **Impact**: This transparency builds trust between consumers and financial institutions, ensuring that people can take control of their financial futures.

    - **Website**: FICO Transparency

2. **Example 2: Google's AI Principles** Google has implemented AI ethics principles that include transparency as a key aspect. For instance, Google explains to users how its AI models work for tasks like image recognition and searches, ensuring that users understand when and why their data is being processed.

   - **Impact**: This helps users feel confident that their data is used responsibly and that they have control over their interactions with the company.

   - **Website**: Google AI Principles

FAQ

Q1: What is the "right to explanation" under data protection laws?
A1: The "right to explanation" allows individuals to receive an understandable explanation of automated decisions that significantly affect them, such as those made by AI. This is required under laws like the **GDPR**, ensuring transparency in how personal data is processed.

Q2: How can AI companies ensure their decisions are explainable to users?
A2: AI companies can use explainability tools like **LIME** or **SHAP**, simplify their explanations into plain language, and offer clear channels for users to inquire about decisions. Additionally, they should proactively disclose when AI is being used in decision-making.

Q3: Why is transparency important in AI systems?
A3: Transparency helps build trust between organizations and their users by ensuring people understand how decisions are made and how their data is used. This is essential for both legal compliance and ethical AI deployment.

MOTD

"Transparency isn't just a requirement; it's the foundation of trust in AI systems. Make every decision clear to your users."

Chapter 7: AI Transparency and Accountability
7.4 The DPO's Role in Promoting Transparency

1. How DPOs Can Push for Clear Communication and Documentation of AI Systems

The **Data Protection Officer (DPO)** plays a crucial role in advocating for transparency in AI systems by ensuring clear communication and thorough documentation. This involves:

- **Clear Communication**: DPOs must work with teams across the organization to ensure AI systems are designed with transparency in mind. This includes documenting the decision-making processes of AI systems, ensuring users understand when AI is used, and how their data is processed.

- **Comprehensive Documentation**: Every step of the AI development process should be clearly documented. This includes maintaining detailed records of AI models, their data sources, and how decisions are made. These records should be accessible during audits and be compliant with legal standards like the **GDPR** and **AI Ethics Guidelines**.

2. Ensuring that Transparency Efforts Align with Legal Requirements

The DPO's role extends to ensuring that transparency efforts comply with all relevant **data protection laws**, particularly:

- **GDPR Compliance**: As per GDPR, organizations must clearly inform individuals about how their data is used by AI. The DPO ensures that these practices are in place by advocating for clear notices and enabling data subject rights, such as the right to explanation.

- **Alignment with Other Legal Standards**: The DPO must also ensure that transparency practices align with emerging AI regulations, such as the **EU Artificial Intelligence Act**. By aligning the AI system's documentation and communication strategies with these legal frameworks, the DPO ensures the organization mitigates potential legal risks.

3. Managing Transparency During AI Audits and Assessments

Audits and assessments of AI systems are vital for ensuring that transparency is maintained over time. During these evaluations:

- **Internal Audits**: DPOs must ensure that internal audits are performed regularly to evaluate if AI systems are maintaining transparency. These audits will assess whether the AI decision-making processes, data collection methods, and user communications meet legal requirements.

- **External Audits**: DPOs also collaborate with external bodies or regulatory authorities to ensure AI systems are transparent. This helps ensure that the

AI's functions can be scrutinized and that stakeholders are reassured that the systems operate fairly.

- **Assessment and Reporting**: The DPO ensures that all audit results and assessments are documented and reported, ensuring clear visibility into how AI systems are functioning and whether they align with transparency standards.

4. Action Point: Incorporate Transparency Audits in AI Development Cycles

To ensure transparency is embedded from the beginning of the AI system's lifecycle:

- **Include Transparency in Development**: During the development phase of AI systems, DPOs should advocate for periodic **transparency audits**. This includes reviewing AI design documents, testing models for bias, and ensuring decision-making processes are clearly documented and communicated.

- **Regular Review**: DPOs should establish a framework where audits are conducted at different stages of the development cycle. This helps identify issues early and ensures transparency is maintained through the AI's entire lifecycle.

- **Building Transparency into the Design**: Collaborate with the engineering and development teams to integrate transparency into AI algorithms. By doing this, the organization avoids reactive efforts and ensures a proactive stance on transparency.

Real-World Examples

1. **Example 1: IBM Watson for Healthcare** IBM's **Watson for Healthcare** is an AI system designed to assist doctors with medical diagnoses. As part of its transparency efforts, IBM documents how Watson makes its recommendations, ensuring that patients and healthcare providers can understand the reasoning behind any medical advice or suggestions provided by the system.

   - **Impact**: By maintaining clear documentation, IBM ensures that both healthcare providers and patients can trust the system's outputs, reducing the risk of misdiagnosis and improving overall healthcare quality.

   - **Website**: IBM Watson Health

2. **Example 2: Microsoft's AI and Transparency** Microsoft has implemented transparency guidelines for its AI systems, including clear communication about how AI systems process data and make decisions. The company

integrates feedback from stakeholders and regularly audits its systems to ensure compliance with data privacy laws and transparency standards.

- o **Impact**: This proactive transparency builds trust with users, especially in sensitive areas like facial recognition or hiring systems.

- o **Website**: Microsoft AI Principles

FAQ

Q1: How can DPOs promote transparency in AI systems?
A1: DPOs can promote transparency by ensuring that AI systems are clearly documented, communicating how AI makes decisions to users, and making sure that all documentation aligns with data protection laws like GDPR. They should also encourage transparency during internal and external audits.

Q2: What role does the DPO play during AI audits?
A2: The DPO ensures that AI audits are conducted to assess transparency and compliance with legal requirements. They play a role in managing both internal and external audits, ensuring that AI decision-making processes are transparent and well-documented.

Q3: Why are transparency audits essential in AI development cycles?
A3: Transparency audits help ensure that AI systems maintain clarity in how data is processed, and decisions are made. These audits help identify and resolve potential issues early in the development cycle, preventing non-compliance and promoting trust.

MOTD

"Transparency in AI is not just a compliance requirement; it's the cornerstone of trust and accountability in technology."

Chapter 7: AI Transparency and Accountability
7.5 Case Studies of Transparent AI Systems

1. Real-World Examples of Successful Transparent AI Practices

Several organizations have demonstrated the positive impact of transparent AI systems, leading to higher levels of trust, compliance, and ethical alignment. Some key examples include:

- **Google's AI Principles**: Google has developed a set of AI principles that govern the use of AI within the company, promoting fairness, accountability, and transparency. Google publicly shares how AI models are trained and used, ensuring users understand the AI's decision-making processes. This openness allows both internal and external stakeholders to scrutinize AI systems for potential biases or ethical concerns.

    - **Impact**: By implementing these principles, Google helps ensure that AI is used responsibly, minimizing negative impacts on users. It also encourages other companies to follow suit, establishing a broader culture of responsible AI development.

    - **Website**: Google AI Principles

- **Netflix's Explainable AI in Content Recommendations**: Netflix has implemented transparent AI systems for its content recommendation engine. The company makes efforts to ensure that users understand how their viewing preferences impact content suggestions. This transparency helps improve user satisfaction and trust in the platform, knowing their data is being used in a meaningful, yet understandable way.

    - **Impact**: Users are more likely to trust the platform and interact more positively when they understand the logic behind personalized recommendations. This not only benefits Netflix in terms of customer retention but also builds brand loyalty.

    - **Website**: Netflix Tech Blog

2. Lessons Learned from Companies that Prioritized Transparency

From these case studies, key lessons can be learned:

- **Clear Communication of AI Decision-Making**: Both Google and Netflix prioritize making AI decisions understandable to users. This transparency enhances user experience and ensures that individuals know how and why their data is being used.

- **Proactive Ethical Frameworks**: Google's AI principles illustrate the importance of embedding ethics into AI from the start. By developing clear guidelines around fairness, transparency, and accountability, organizations can avoid risks associated with AI-driven discrimination and privacy violations.

- **Continuous Monitoring and Adjustment**: Netflix's approach to explainable AI also demonstrates the value of ongoing monitoring of AI models to ensure they stay aligned with user expectations and privacy concerns. Regular updates to the transparency of AI systems help address any emerging issues.

3. How to Implement Transparent AI Practices in Your Own Organization

To implement transparent AI practices, organizations should:

- **Document All AI Decision-Making Processes**: Every AI system should have clear documentation that explains how it works, the data it uses, and how decisions are made.

- **Engage with Stakeholders**: Transparency should not only be an internal practice but also involve engaging with end-users and external stakeholders, ensuring that everyone understands how AI operates and how it affects them.

- **Regularly Audit and Update AI Systems**: Transparency is not a one-time activity. Regular audits, assessments, and updates should be conducted to maintain the ethical alignment and transparency of AI systems.

4. Action Point: Apply Lessons from Successful Case Studies to Improve Your Own AI Transparency Efforts

Use the lessons from Google, Netflix, and other successful case studies to inform your own AI transparency practices:

- **Establish Clear AI Guidelines**: Develop your own ethical AI guidelines that emphasize transparency and accountability.

- **Create Easy-to-Understand Explanations**: Ensure that end-users and stakeholders can easily understand how AI makes decisions and the data it uses.

- **Monitor and Evolve**: Be proactive in monitoring your AI systems and continuously improve transparency through regular audits and updates.

Real-World Examples

1. **Example 1: Google's AI Principles** Google's publicly available AI principles focus on transparency and fairness, offering clear explanations of how its AI systems are designed and deployed. This not only helps the company stay compliant with global regulations like GDPR but also earns public trust.

- o **Impact**: By establishing clear AI guidelines, Google ensures responsible AI use, reducing the risk of public backlash and increasing overall user trust.

  - o **Website**: Google AI Principles

2. **Example 2: Netflix's Personalized Recommendations** Netflix's AI systems for content recommendation are designed to be transparent, offering users insights into why certain shows or movies are recommended. This transparency strengthens user engagement and trust.

   - o **Impact**: Users feel more confident about their data usage, and the platform benefits from improved retention and personalized experiences.

   - o **Website**: Netflix Tech Blog

FAQ

Q1: Why is transparency in AI so important?
A1: Transparency in AI ensures users understand how their data is being used and how decisions are made. This builds trust, minimizes the risk of ethical violations, and helps organizations comply with laws like GDPR.

Q2: How can my organization implement transparent AI practices?
A2: Start by documenting how your AI systems work, explaining decision-making processes clearly, and engaging users in understanding these systems. Regular audits and updates are also crucial to maintain transparency.

Q3: What are the benefits of transparent AI systems?
A3: Transparent AI systems lead to greater trust from users, improved customer satisfaction, legal compliance, and better overall management of data privacy risks. This transparency also fosters ethical practices in AI development.

MOTD

"Transparency in AI is more than just good practice—it's the foundation of trust and ethical responsibility in the digital age."

Chapter 8: Handling Data Breaches in the Age of AI

8.1 Common Causes of Data Breaches in AI Systems

1. AI Vulnerabilities: From Algorithmic Biases to Insecure Data Storage

AI systems are often built on vast amounts of data, and any vulnerabilities in these systems can lead to significant data breaches. Two major types of vulnerabilities include:

- **Algorithmic Biases**: AI algorithms, if not properly trained or monitored, can inadvertently make biased decisions, leading to unintentional leakage or misuse of personal data. For example, facial recognition algorithms may misidentify certain demographic groups more than others, exposing their data to inaccurate profiling.

  - **Example**: In 2018, the *Amazon Recognition* system, used by law enforcement agencies, showed significant bias, misidentifying people of color more frequently than white individuals, leading to privacy concerns and legal implications.

  - **Impact**: The algorithmic bias increased the risk of unjust surveillance and discriminatory practices. It also sparked widespread concerns about the ethical use of AI, forcing Amazon to halt certain collaborations and initiate bias audits.

- **Insecure Data Storage**: AI systems often rely on huge datasets, and poor security practices during data storage or transmission can expose these datasets to unauthorized access. Data encryption and secure storage methods are essential to prevent such breaches.

  - **Example**: In 2019, *First American Financial Corporation* experienced a data breach where over 800 million documents containing sensitive information were exposed due to inadequate security protocols on their AI-powered document-sharing platform.

  - **Impact**: This breach highlighted the risks AI systems can pose when data is not properly secured, leading to public backlash and a loss of trust.

2. Human Error and Lack of Compliance with Data Protection Standards

Despite technological advancements, human error remains a primary cause of data breaches in AI systems. Common mistakes include misconfigurations, improper access controls, or failure to apply critical security patches. When individuals lack awareness or training on data protection standards, AI systems become more vulnerable.

- **Example**: In 2017, a misconfigured *Amazon Web Services* (AWS) cloud storage instance exposed data from over 14 million customers of *Accenture—* an example of how human negligence and a failure to follow compliance standards led to a large-scale breach.

  - **Impact**: This breach not only resulted in financial losses but also hurt Accenture's reputation as it raised questions about how securely AI-powered systems handle sensitive customer information.

3. Breaches Resulting from Third-Party Collaborations or Data Sharing

When AI systems rely on third-party vendors or partners for data sharing, this opens up potential vulnerability points. Any breach in the supply chain can lead to a cascading effect on data security. Third-party vendors may not always have the same data protection standards, leading to vulnerabilities.

- **Example**: The *Facebook-Cambridge Analytica scandal* of 2018 involved the misuse of personal data through a third-party app, which was used to harvest personal information from millions of Facebook users without their consent.

  - **Impact**: The scandal exposed how AI and big data systems can be manipulated by third-party collaborations, leading to an erosion of public trust and resulting in heavy fines for Facebook under GDPR regulations.

  - **Website**: Cambridge Analytica Scandal Overview

4. Action Point: Regularly Review AI Systems for Potential Breach Points

To mitigate the risk of data breaches, it's crucial for organizations to:

- **Conduct Regular Audits**: Perform regular security audits of both AI models and their underlying data infrastructures to identify vulnerabilities before they are exploited.

- **Implement Access Controls**: Ensure strict access control protocols are in place to limit who can access sensitive data and AI systems.

- **Update Compliance Protocols**: Stay up to date with data protection regulations such as GDPR and CCPA to ensure AI systems are fully compliant and secure.

Real-World Examples

1. **Amazon Recognition Bias (2018)**
   Amazon's AI-powered facial recognition software faced criticism due to algorithmic biases that misidentified people, particularly people of color. This

raised privacy concerns regarding AI's role in surveillance, leading to scrutiny and a review of Amazon's policies.

- o **Impact**: Demonstrated the importance of addressing biases and ensuring fairness in AI models.

- o **Website**: Amazon Rekognition

2. **First American Financial Data Breach (2019)**
   A breach exposed millions of sensitive documents due to poor security practices on the AI-powered platform used by First American. It served as a cautionary tale for the importance of secure data storage.

- o **Impact**: Highlighted how AI systems need to incorporate robust security measures to protect sensitive data.

- o **Website**: First American Data Breach

FAQ

Q1: How can AI systems contribute to data breaches?
A1: AI systems can contribute to data breaches through algorithmic biases, insecure data storage, human error, and third-party vulnerabilities. Regular audits and compliance with data protection standards can help mitigate these risks.

Q2: What role does human error play in AI-related data breaches?
A2: Human error, such as misconfigurations, lack of training, or negligence in applying security measures, is a common cause of AI-related data breaches. Ensuring adequate staff training and adherence to security protocols can reduce such risks.

Q3: What steps can organizations take to avoid data breaches in AI systems?
A3: Organizations should regularly audit their AI systems, implement strong data encryption and access controls, and ensure compliance with data protection laws like GDPR. Collaboration with third-party vendors should also include thorough security checks.

MOTD

"Proactive risk management and transparency are key to preventing AI data breaches. Secure your systems today to protect tomorrow's data."

Chapter 8: Handling Data Breaches in the Age of AI
8.2 Procedures for Managing AI Data Breaches

1. Step-by-Step Process for Responding to AI Data Breaches

When a data breach occurs within an AI system, there's a structured process that should be followed to mitigate damage and ensure compliance with relevant laws:

- **Detection**: The first step is to identify the breach quickly. This requires effective monitoring and logging systems to detect unauthorized access or data leaks in real-time.

- **Containment**: Once detected, immediate action must be taken to contain the breach, preventing further access to sensitive data. This could include shutting down compromised systems or isolating them from the rest of the network.

- **Assessment**: Assess the severity and scope of the breach. What data has been compromised? Who are the affected individuals? Understanding the impact is crucial for next steps.

- **Notification**: After containment and assessment, the next step is to notify the relevant stakeholders (regulators, affected individuals, internal teams).

- **Remediation**: Finally, address the root cause of the breach. This could involve patching security vulnerabilities, updating encryption protocols, or retraining the AI system if the breach is algorithm-related.

2. How to Notify Regulators and Affected Individuals in Compliance with GDPR

Under the **General Data Protection Regulation (GDPR)**, organizations must notify regulators within 72 hours of discovering a breach if personal data is involved. They must also inform affected individuals without undue delay if their rights are at risk.

- **Notification to Regulators**: Notify the relevant authority (e.g., the Information Commissioner's Office in the UK) using the breach notification form provided by the regulatory body.

- **Notification to Affected Individuals**: If the breach is likely to result in high risk to individuals, you must notify them directly, providing clear information about what happened, the potential consequences, and what they can do to protect themselves.

3. The Importance of Transparency During a Breach Crisis

Transparency is vital during a breach crisis. Clear communication helps maintain trust with affected individuals and regulators. Transparency includes:

- **Public Announcements**: Be honest and clear about the scope of the breach, its potential impact, and the steps taken to address it.

- **Ongoing Updates**: Provide updates as you continue to investigate the breach and take corrective actions.

- **Future Prevention**: Share what steps will be taken to prevent a similar breach in the future, which can demonstrate the organization's commitment to data security.

Real-World Examples

1. **Equifax Data Breach (2017)**
   In 2017, the credit reporting agency **Equifax** experienced a massive data breach where hackers exploited a vulnerability in a web application framework. The breach affected around 147 million Americans, exposing personal data like social security numbers, addresses, and birth dates.

   - **Impact**: Equifax faced criticism for its delayed response, including a failure to notify affected individuals immediately. The company was fined $700 million to settle lawsuits and regulatory actions.

   - **Website**: Equifax Data Breach Settlement

2. **Facebook Data Breach (2018)**
   In 2018, Facebook suffered a breach that exposed the personal data of over 50 million users due to a vulnerability in its "View As" feature.

   - **Impact**: Facebook notified affected users within days, and the company was investigated for non-compliance with GDPR. They faced a $5 billion fine from the U.S. Federal Trade Commission.

   - **Website**: Facebook Data Breach Details

Checklist for AI Data Breach Response

Step	Action	Responsible Party	Timeline
Detection	Monitor for irregular activity	Security Team	Real-time
Containment	Isolate affected systems	IT Department	Immediately
Assessment	Evaluate the scope of the breach	Data Protection Officer	Within 24 hours
Notification	Notify regulators and individuals	DPO, Legal Team	Within 72 hours

Step	Action	Responsible Party	Timeline
Remediation	Address root cause (patch, retrain)	IT & AI Development Team	Within 1 week

FAQ

Q1: How quickly must I notify regulators about a data breach under GDPR?
A1: Under GDPR, you must notify the relevant regulatory authority within 72 hours of discovering a breach if personal data is involved.

Q2: What should I include in the notification to affected individuals?
A2: The notification should include details of the breach, the type of data affected, potential consequences, and steps the individuals can take to protect themselves.

Q3: Why is transparency important during an AI data breach?
A3: Transparency builds trust with users and regulators. It shows that the organization is handling the situation responsibly and is taking steps to prevent future breaches.

MOTD

"A data breach is not just a technical issue—it's a trust issue. Be transparent, act quickly, and always prioritize security."

Chapter 8: Handling Data Breaches in the Age of AI
8.3 Preventative Measures and Best Practices

1. Implementing Strong Security Measures in AI Systems

To safeguard AI systems from data breaches, it's essential to implement robust security measures right from the design phase. Key steps include:

- **Encryption**: Ensure that both data at rest (stored data) and data in transit (data being transmitted) are encrypted using strong algorithms. This reduces the risk of unauthorized access during transmission or while data is stored.

- **Access Control**: Implement strong user authentication (multi-factor authentication or MFA) and fine-grained access control policies. Limit access to sensitive data and AI models to only those who need it.

- **Data Anonymization**: Where possible, anonymize sensitive data used in AI training and operations. This ensures that even if data is leaked, it cannot be easily traced back to individuals.

2. Conducting Regular Vulnerability Assessments and Penetration Testing

Routine security testing is crucial for identifying vulnerabilities within AI systems before attackers can exploit them. These proactive measures include:

- **Vulnerability Scanning**: Use automated tools to scan your systems for known security vulnerabilities. Regular scanning ensures that new threats are identified and patched quickly.

- **Penetration Testing**: Simulate an attack on your AI systems to identify potential entry points and weak spots. Pen testing mimics the tactics of malicious actors to evaluate the resilience of your systems.

- **AI-Specific Testing**: AI systems have unique risks, such as adversarial attacks where small changes to input data can mislead models. Testing AI algorithms specifically for such vulnerabilities is critical.

3. Best Practices for Third-Party Data Sharing and AI Partnerships

AI systems often rely on third-party data and partnerships, making it essential to establish strong security practices in these collaborations:

- **Data Sharing Agreements**: Establish clear agreements that outline data protection responsibilities, security requirements, and breach protocols.

- **Third-Party Risk Assessments**: Conduct due diligence and risk assessments on third-party vendors or collaborators to ensure they have adequate security measures in place.

- **Continuous Monitoring**: Regularly audit third-party AI models, data access logs, and systems to ensure compliance with security standards and regulations.

Real-World Examples

1. **Tesla's AI and Data Security Practices**
   Tesla, known for using AI in its self-driving cars, has made security a top priority in its AI systems. The company implements end-to-end encryption in its vehicles' data communications, and its AI models are continuously monitored for vulnerabilities. Additionally, Tesla conducts regular penetration tests and vulnerability assessments to stay ahead of potential threats.

   - **Impact**: Tesla's proactive approach helps mitigate the risks of data breaches or malicious attacks on their AI-driven systems.

   - **Website**: Tesla Security

2. **Uber's Third-Party Data Sharing Practices**
   Uber, when partnering with third-party services to optimize its ride-sharing algorithms, ensures that they have stringent data-sharing agreements and security checks in place. They ensure the third-party vendors comply with industry best practices in data protection, and Uber conducts regular audits on its third-party relationships to avoid data leakage.

   - **Impact**: This helps Uber maintain control over sensitive customer data and prevent breaches through third-party vendors.

   - **Website**: Uber Security

Checklist for Preventing Data Breaches in AI Systems

Action	Description	Responsible Party	Frequency
Encryption	Implement encryption for data at rest and in transit	IT & Security Team	Ongoing
Access Control	Use MFA and access policies to limit data access	IT & Security Team	Ongoing
Vulnerability Scanning	Regularly scan for vulnerabilities in AI systems	Security Team	Monthly
Penetration Testing	Simulate attacks to identify weaknesses	Security Team	Quarterly

Action	Description	Responsible Party	Frequency
Third-Party Audits	Evaluate the security practices of third-party vendors	Procurement & Legal Teams	Annually

FAQ

Q1: Why is encryption so important for AI systems?
A1: Encryption ensures that sensitive data is unreadable to unauthorized users, even if a breach occurs. It protects data during storage and while being transmitted, reducing the chances of exploitation.

Q2: How often should penetration testing be conducted on AI systems?
A2: Penetration testing should be done at least quarterly to identify and address vulnerabilities before they can be exploited. However, it should be more frequent if the AI system is exposed to high-risk environments.

Q3: What role do third-party vendors play in data breaches in AI systems?
A3: Third-party vendors can be a significant risk if their security practices are not properly assessed. It's important to have clear data-sharing agreements and conduct regular audits to ensure they adhere to security standards.

MOTD

"Prevention is always better than cure. Secure your AI systems now to avoid tomorrow's data breach."

1. The DPO's Role in Detecting, Managing, and Reporting AI Data Breaches

As the designated Data Protection Officer (DPO), you are at the forefront of managing AI-related data breaches. Your responsibilities include:

- **Detection**: Implement systems for detecting data breaches as early as possible. In AI systems, this might involve monitoring for unusual patterns, unexpected data flows, or unauthorized access. Using AI and machine learning models to predict or identify anomalies is a proactive way to spot breaches before they escalate.

- **Management**: Once a breach is detected, the DPO is responsible for activating the breach response plan, coordinating resources, and managing internal teams. This includes determining the scope of the breach, containing the affected systems, and preventing further data loss.

- **Reporting**: Under regulations like GDPR, data breaches must be reported within 72 hours. The DPO plays a crucial role in preparing detailed reports, including the nature of the breach, affected data, and measures taken to mitigate the issue. Clear documentation ensures compliance and helps inform stakeholders.

2. How to Effectively Communicate Breach Information to Stakeholders

Communication during a data breach is critical. As a DPO, you must:

- **Internal Communication**: Inform key stakeholders, including the legal team, management, and IT staff. This ensures everyone understands the gravity of the situation and the steps required.

- **External Communication**: If personal data is affected, notify the individuals impacted by the breach, explaining what happened, what data was involved, and what actions they can take. Additionally, regulators must be notified, including details of the breach and corrective actions taken.

- **Transparency**: During any breach, especially with AI systems, transparency is key. Keeping stakeholders informed helps manage trust and reputational risks.

3. Reviewing Breach Cases and Improving Future AI Data Handling

After the breach is resolved, it is essential for the DPO to conduct a thorough post-breach review. This includes:

- **Post-Mortem Analysis**: Analyze how the breach occurred, whether it was due to human error, technical failure, or insufficient security protocols.

- **Updating Protocols**: Based on findings, update security measures, training programs, and risk management frameworks to prevent future breaches.

- **Continuous Improvement**: Leverage lessons learned to create stronger preventive measures and improve AI data handling practices.

Real-World Examples

1. **British Airways Data Breach (2018)**
   British Airways suffered a major breach when attackers intercepted customer data from their website and mobile app. As the DPO, handling this breach involved quickly identifying the scope, notifying affected individuals, and reporting the incident to the Information Commissioner's Office (ICO). They also had to work with third-party vendors to ensure better security moving forward.

   - **Impact**: British Airways faced a £183 million fine for GDPR violations. However, by acting swiftly and being transparent, they minimized further damage.

   - **Website**: British Airways Incident

2. **Facebook's Cambridge Analytica Scandal (2018)**
   While not a typical data breach, the Facebook-Cambridge Analytica case involved unauthorized access to personal data through a third-party application. The DPO had to handle massive media scrutiny and navigate complex regulatory responses, all while communicating to users about what data was involved and the steps being taken.

   - **Impact**: Facebook faced regulatory fines and a loss of trust. However, this event led them to improve transparency and data protection practices moving forward.

   - **Website**: Facebook Data Scandal

Checklist for DPOs in Managing AI Data Breaches

Action	Description	Responsible Party	Frequency
Detection Systems	Implement AI-based anomaly detection tools	IT & Security Teams	Ongoing
Breach Response Plan	Activate breach response and containment protocol	DPO & Incident Response	As needed

Action	Description	Responsible Party	Frequency
Internal Communication	Inform key internal stakeholders promptly	DPO	Ongoing
External Notification	Notify regulators and affected individuals	DPO	Within 72 hours
Post-Breach Review	Conduct a thorough review and update protocols	DPO & Security Team	After every breach

FAQ

Q1: What should be the first step when a breach is detected in an AI system?
A1: The first step is to contain the breach to prevent further data loss. This may involve disconnecting affected systems from the network and securing sensitive data until further analysis can be conducted.

Q2: How should DPOs communicate a breach to affected individuals?
A2: DPOs should send clear, concise notifications explaining the nature of the breach, the type of data affected, the potential risks, and the steps individuals can take to protect themselves.

Q3: What are some key takeaways from handling a breach to improve future AI systems?
A3: Key takeaways include identifying gaps in security, improving employee training, updating security protocols, and enhancing transparency measures to avoid similar issues in the future.

MOTD

"Data protection is not just about compliance—it's about building trust through transparency and accountability."

Chapter 8: Handling Data Breaches in the Age of AI
8.5 Legal and Ethical Considerations in Breach Response

1. Balancing Legal Requirements with Ethical Considerations During Breach Management

When managing a data breach, the primary focus is often on legal compliance. However, ethical considerations play a crucial role in shaping the response.

- **Legal Requirements**: Regulations like the GDPR (General Data Protection Regulation) mandate strict timelines and procedures for notifying both regulators and affected individuals. Failure to comply can result in hefty fines and loss of credibility. Legal requirements typically focus on transparency, timelines (e.g., notifying within 72 hours), and remedial actions such as offering affected individuals access to identity theft protection services.

- **Ethical Considerations**: Ethically, organizations must go beyond merely fulfilling legal obligations. Transparency, respect for affected individuals, and proactive steps to prevent future breaches are key ethical practices. Being open about the breach and offering resources like credit monitoring or support hotlines enhances the organization's reputation and shows respect for the individuals whose data was compromised.

2. How to Ensure Proper Notification and Remedy for Affected Individuals

It's not enough to simply notify individuals about a breach. It's vital that organizations offer clear, helpful, and actionable information to affected individuals:

- **Clear Notification**: The breach notification should clearly explain what happened, the data involved, potential risks, and what actions individuals should take. Avoiding legal jargon and using plain language ensures that individuals understand the gravity of the situation.

- **Remedial Actions**: Offer remedial measures like credit monitoring, support for filing complaints, or refunds for any losses incurred due to the breach. These actions not only comply with legal requirements but also signal an ethical commitment to helping affected individuals recover.

3. Learning from Past Breaches to Reduce the Likelihood of Future Incidents

After handling a data breach, organizations must conduct a **post-breach analysis**. This includes identifying the root cause of the breach and implementing measures to prevent future occurrences:

- **Root Cause Analysis**: Review what went wrong—was it a technical vulnerability, human error, or lack of compliance?

- **Proactive Measures**: Strengthen security measures, implement better training programs for employees, and improve data protection policies. By learning from past incidents, you can build a more resilient system that better protects users and prevents data breaches in the future.

Real-World Examples

1. **Equifax Data Breach (2017)**
   In one of the most infamous breaches, Equifax exposed the personal information of 147 million people. Ethically, the company's response faced criticism for the slow notification of affected individuals. However, legally, they complied with U.S. laws by offering free credit monitoring and identity theft protection to impacted customers.

   - **Impact**: The breach led to a $700 million settlement and significant damage to Equifax's reputation.
   - **Website**: Equifax Data Breach

2. **Target Data Breach (2013)**
   Target experienced a data breach where hackers stole personal and financial information from 40 million credit and debit card accounts. They were legally required to notify customers, but they also took ethical steps by offering free credit monitoring and other protective measures to affected individuals.

   - **Impact**: The breach cost Target $162 million in direct costs, and led to a tarnished reputation, but their ethical response helped restore trust.
   - **Website**: Target Data Breach Details

Checklist for DPOs to Ensure Legal & Ethical Compliance in Breach Response

Action	Description	Responsible Party	Frequency
Legal Notification	Notify regulators and affected individuals within the mandated time frame (e.g., 72 hours under GDPR)	DPO & Legal Team	As needed
Clear Communication	Communicate the breach details in plain language with actionable steps for affected individuals	DPO & PR Team	As needed
Ethical Remediation	Offer support services like credit monitoring or free services to mitigate the breach's impact	DPO & Customer Service	As needed

Action	Description	Responsible Party	Frequency
Root Cause Analysis	Review how the breach happened and identify security or process gaps	DPO & Security Team	After every breach
Security Improvements	Implement stronger security protocols and data protection policies to avoid future breaches	DPO & IT Team	Ongoing

FAQ

Q1: What should be the ethical considerations when notifying individuals about a data breach?
A1: Ethical considerations include ensuring that individuals receive clear, comprehensible information about what data was affected, potential risks, and the steps they can take to protect themselves. Offering remedial measures like credit monitoring shows a commitment to helping those impacted.

Q2: How can companies prevent future data breaches based on past incidents?
A2: After each breach, companies should conduct a thorough review to identify weaknesses. Strengthening security measures, conducting employee training, and improving internal policies can significantly reduce the risk of future incidents.

Q3: What role does the DPO play in balancing legal and ethical responses to a data breach?
A3: The DPO ensures compliance with legal requirements, like timely notifications, while also advocating for ethical practices, such as transparent communication, offering support to affected individuals, and implementing measures to prevent future breaches.

MOTD

"Every breach is an opportunity to strengthen your security, grow your trust, and become more resilient."

Chapter 9: DPOs and AI Data Ethics in Practice

9.1 Real-World Examples of DPOs in AI Ethics Roles

1. Case Studies of Organizations Where DPOs Shaped AI Ethics Practices

Data Protection Officers (DPOs) play an essential role in shaping the ethical use of AI systems. Here are some examples where DPOs helped integrate ethical considerations into AI practices:

- **Example 1: The European Commission's AI Ethics Guidelines**
  In 2019, the European Commission's DPO played a significant role in shaping the ethical guidelines for AI deployment. The DPO helped ensure that AI systems being developed and implemented by various departments were aligned with the EU's ethical standards, focusing on fairness, transparency, and privacy protection.

  - **Impact**: The guidelines led to a more responsible approach to AI development across Europe, setting global standards for AI ethics and data protection.

  - **Website**: European Commission AI Guidelines

- **Example 2: Microsoft's AI and Ethics Framework**
  Microsoft's DPOs are pivotal in their responsible AI initiatives. Microsoft integrated a comprehensive AI ethics framework that includes transparency, accountability, and data protection principles into their product design. The DPO guided the company in establishing mechanisms for ongoing ethics reviews and impact assessments of AI systems.

  - **Impact**: This proactive approach resulted in Microsoft becoming a leader in the ethical deployment of AI, with AI systems that ensure privacy and minimize bias.

  - **Website**: Microsoft AI Ethics Framework

2. Success Stories Where DPOs Played a Key Role in Responsible AI

- **Example 3: The Role of DPOs in Healthcare AI (e.g., NHS)**
  In healthcare, where AI applications are increasingly used for diagnosis and treatment, the role of DPOs is crucial. The NHS in the UK used its DPOs to guide AI adoption in a way that respects patient privacy while ensuring AI algorithms are both accurate and fair. DPOs were instrumental in making sure that AI-driven health tools met legal requirements and maintained the highest ethical standards.

  - **Impact**: By ensuring transparency in AI-powered health tools and guiding them through GDPR compliance, the NHS helped build trust with patients and healthcare professionals alike.

o **Website**: NHS AI Adoption

3. Common Mistakes to Avoid in AI Data Protection

- **Overlooking Bias in Data**: One of the most common mistakes organizations make is neglecting to address biases present in the data used to train AI models. DPOs should ensure that any data used is representative, fair, and diverse.

- **Lack of Transparency**: Failing to explain AI decisions clearly to end-users is another mistake. DPOs must advocate for clear communication of how AI systems make decisions, ensuring that users understand the logic behind automated actions.

- **Ignoring Regular Audits**: Data protection isn't a one-time event; AI systems must be constantly monitored and audited. DPOs must implement ongoing assessments to detect and address vulnerabilities in AI models and data-handling practices.

Checklist for DPOs in AI Ethics Roles

Action	Description	Responsible Party	Frequency
Bias Detection in Data	Assess data used for AI systems for potential biases.	DPO & Data Science Teams	Ongoing
Transparency Measures	Ensure clear communication about how AI systems operate.	DPO & PR Teams	During AI Development & Deployment
Ethical Audits	Regular audits to review AI systems for compliance with ethical standards.	DPO & Compliance Teams	Quarterly
Training on AI Ethics	Train employees on the ethical considerations in AI development.	DPO & HR	Annual
Collaboration with AI Governance Teams	Work with AI development teams to align AI projects with ethical frameworks.	DPO & Development Teams	Continuous

FAQ

Q1: How can DPOs contribute to minimizing bias in AI systems?
A1: DPOs can ensure that the data used to train AI models is diverse and representative of all relevant demographics. They also advocate for fairness assessments and work with AI development teams to identify and correct biases.

Q2: What are the most common ethical mistakes that DPOs should avoid in AI implementation?
A2: The most common ethical mistakes include neglecting to address biases in AI data, failing to provide clear explanations for AI decisions to end-users, and overlooking the need for regular audits to ensure compliance with data protection standards.

Q3: How does the role of DPOs in AI ethics differ from traditional data protection?
A3: Unlike traditional data protection, DPOs in AI ethics focus not just on legal compliance but also on ensuring that AI systems respect human rights, fairness, transparency, and accountability. They also assess the broader social and ethical implications of AI deployment.

MOTD

"Ethical AI is not just a goal; it's a continuous journey led by responsible leadership."

Chapter 9: DPOs and AI Data Ethics in Practice
9.2 Case Studies of AI Implementation and Data Protection Failures

1. High-Profile Failures in AI and the Data Protection Lessons Learned

AI-driven systems have the potential to transform industries, but when improperly implemented, they can lead to catastrophic data protection failures. Here are a few examples of high-profile failures:

- **Example 1: The Cambridge Analytica Scandal**
  The Cambridge Analytica scandal revealed how AI algorithms could be used to manipulate data and influence political decisions. AI systems were used to harvest data from millions of Facebook users without their consent, breaching privacy regulations and violating data protection laws.

  - **Impact**: This failure led to Facebook being fined $5 billion by the FTC and damaged its reputation. It also prompted legislative changes and heightened scrutiny on AI systems used in data harvesting.

  - **Lessons Learned**: Organizations must ensure that they have strong data governance frameworks in place, avoid unauthorized data collection, and prioritize user consent.

  - **Website**: Cambridge Analytica Scandal Details

- **Example 2: Amazon's AI Recruiting Tool Bias**
  Amazon's AI-driven recruitment tool was found to exhibit bias against female candidates. The system was trained on resumes submitted to the company, which were predominantly from male applicants, leading to a bias against women applicants for technical roles.

  - **Impact**: The tool was scrapped after it was found to discriminate, and Amazon faced backlash for failing to properly test for bias in its AI systems.

  - **Lessons Learned**: This failure highlights the need for continuous testing for fairness and equity in AI systems, particularly in sensitive areas like hiring.

  - **Website**: Amazon AI Bias Article

2. How Data Breaches or Unethical AI Practices Impact Businesses and Individuals

When AI systems fail or are misused, the impact on both businesses and individuals can be severe:

- **For Businesses**: Financial penalties, such as fines from regulatory bodies like the GDPR or FTC, loss of consumer trust, and the costs of fixing the issues can severely damage a company's bottom line. Additionally, long-term reputational damage can make it difficult for a business to recover.

- **For Individuals**: Data breaches and unethical AI practices can lead to privacy violations, discrimination, and loss of personal data. Affected individuals may suffer from identity theft, financial losses, or unfair treatment based on biased AI decisions.

3. What DPOs Can Do to Prevent Such Failures

Data Protection Officers (DPOs) have a pivotal role in preventing AI-related data protection failures:

- **Implementing Strong Data Governance**: DPOs must ensure that AI systems are built with strong data protection measures. This includes anonymizing personal data, obtaining proper user consent, and conducting regular privacy impact assessments.

- **Regular Audits and Bias Detection**: DPOs should ensure that AI systems undergo continuous auditing and bias detection. Identifying biases early in the development process can prevent future discrimination issues like those faced by Amazon.

- **Training and Awareness**: DPOs should promote training across the organization to raise awareness of data protection principles and the ethical implications of AI. This proactive approach can prevent future data protection failures.

- **Engaging with Stakeholders**: DPOs must be actively involved in communicating with both internal and external stakeholders about the importance of ethical AI practices, building trust, and addressing concerns.

Checklist for DPOs to Prevent AI Data Protection Failures

Action	Description	Responsible Party	Frequency
Data Governance Framework	Implement and maintain a robust data governance framework.	DPO & Legal Teams	Continuous
Bias Testing in AI Systems	Regularly test AI systems for biases, especially in sensitive areas (e.g., hiring).	DPO & AI Teams	Bi-Annual

Action	Description	Responsible Party	Frequency
Privacy Impact Assessments (PIAs)	Conduct PIAs for all AI systems before deployment.	DPO & Privacy Teams	At Development
Compliance Audits	Perform regular audits to ensure AI systems are GDPR-compliant.	DPO & Compliance Teams	Quarterly
Stakeholder Communication	Engage with stakeholders about AI ethics and data protection.	DPO & Communication Teams	Monthly

FAQ

Q1: How can DPOs ensure ethical AI practices in recruitment systems?
A1: DPOs should ensure that AI recruitment tools are regularly audited for bias, particularly in areas like gender, race, and disability. They should also ensure the data used for training the system is diverse and representative of the candidate pool.

Q2: What can DPOs learn from the Cambridge Analytica scandal?
A2: DPOs should learn the importance of securing user consent for data collection and use, maintaining transparency with users about how their data will be used, and ensuring that AI-driven data collection aligns with data protection regulations.

Q3: How do AI failures impact businesses and individuals differently?
A3: Businesses face financial penalties, reputational damage, and legal consequences, while individuals suffer from potential privacy violations, discrimination, and loss of personal data, which can lead to identity theft or unfair treatment.

MOTD

"Learning from past mistakes is the first step toward building a better, more ethical AI future."

Chapter 9: DPOs and AI Data Ethics in Practice
9.3 Lessons Learned from Successes and Failures

1. Key Takeaways from Successful AI Data Protection Initiatives

Successful AI data protection initiatives provide essential insights into how AI systems can be developed and deployed ethically. Here are key takeaways:

- **Example 1: IBM's AI Fairness 360 Toolkit**
  IBM introduced the **AI Fairness 360 Toolkit**, an open-source software designed to help data scientists and AI practitioners detect and mitigate biases in AI models. This initiative reflects IBM's commitment to ethical AI by integrating fairness into AI development from the beginning.

  - **Impact**: The toolkit has been adopted by various organizations, leading to more transparent and equitable AI systems. By proactively addressing bias, companies can prevent the ethical and legal issues that have plagued other AI deployments.

  - **Website**: IBM AI Fairness 360

- **Example 2: Microsoft's AI Ethics Board**
  Microsoft established an **AI and Ethics in Engineering and Research (AETHER) Committee** to guide the development of responsible AI systems. This committee ensures that ethical considerations, such as fairness, accountability, transparency, and privacy, are baked into all of Microsoft's AI projects.

  - **Impact**: This commitment to ethics has fostered public trust and helped Microsoft navigate regulatory scrutiny, making them a leader in AI responsibility.

  - **Website**: Microsoft AI Ethics

2. The Role of Strong Leadership in Driving Ethical AI Practices

Leadership plays a critical role in ensuring that AI systems are developed with a strong ethical foundation:

- **Visionary Leadership**: Leaders who prioritize ethical AI and data protection set a clear direction for the company, aligning technological innovation with ethical principles. They must push for a culture of transparency, fairness, and accountability.

- **Example**: **Sundar Pichai**, CEO of Google, emphasized **AI for Good** in the company's initiatives. By setting ethical guidelines for AI development, he has positioned Google to address concerns about bias, privacy, and societal impact.

- o **Impact**: Ethical leadership helped Google avoid serious ethical dilemmas, building public trust and ensuring that AI technologies are beneficial to society.

3. Creating a Culture of Responsibility and Continuous Improvement in AI Development

AI systems are never "set and forget." Ethical AI requires continuous effort:

- **Ongoing Audits and Reviews**: Regular audits of AI systems, focusing on performance, fairness, and compliance, are essential. DPOs can drive continuous improvement by identifying areas where systems need to be adjusted to comply with emerging regulations or to address unanticipated ethical issues.

- **Employee Engagement**: Leaders must encourage a culture where every team member, from engineers to data scientists, feels accountable for the ethical impact of their work. Providing ongoing training and ensuring awareness of ethical AI guidelines is key to this approach.

4. Action Point: Apply These Lessons to Create a More Robust AI Ethics Framework in Your Organization

- **Step 1**: Build or refine your AI ethics framework, incorporating lessons from successful case studies like IBM's fairness toolkit or Microsoft's AI ethics board.

- **Step 2**: Ensure leadership is committed to AI ethics and actively champions the cause.

- **Step 3**: Establish a culture of continuous improvement, where audits, reviews, and employee engagement are prioritized.

Checklist for Creating a Robust AI Ethics Framework

Action	Description	Responsible Party	Frequency
AI Ethics Framework Development	Develop or update an ethical framework for AI development.	DPO, Leadership Team	Annually
Leadership Commitment	Ensure executives are publicly committed to AI ethics.	CEO, DPO	Ongoing

Action	Description	Responsible Party	Frequency
Regular AI Audits	Conduct regular audits to check AI performance and fairness.	AI Teams, DPO	Quarterly
Employee Training	Provide ongoing training on AI ethics to all employees.	HR, DPO	Bi-Annual
Public Transparency Reports	Share findings and improvements in AI ethics with stakeholders.	Communications, DPO	Annually

FAQ

Q1: How can DPOs influence AI ethics in an organization?
A1: DPOs can influence AI ethics by ensuring that data protection and privacy principles are integrated into AI development processes, advocating for regular audits, and fostering a culture of transparency and responsibility within the company.

Q2: Why is leadership crucial in driving ethical AI practices?
A2: Leadership is crucial because it sets the tone for organizational priorities. Ethical leadership ensures that AI projects align with values such as fairness, transparency, and accountability, which builds public trust and prevents ethical failures.

Q3: What are the key components of a successful AI ethics framework?
A3: A successful AI ethics framework should include policies for data governance, fairness, transparency, privacy protection, continuous auditing, and employee engagement. It should also be aligned with legal regulations such as GDPR.

MOTD

"Ethical AI is not just a regulatory requirement; it's a responsibility to create a future where technology benefits everyone."

Chapter 9: DPOs and AI Data Ethics in Practice
9.4 The DPO as a Strategic Partner in AI Projects

1. Positioning the DPO as a Trusted Advisor in AI Initiatives

The role of the **Data Protection Officer (DPO)** in AI projects is far from just ensuring compliance; the DPO should be seen as a **trusted advisor** from the very beginning. As AI systems can often present complex challenges in terms of data privacy, security, and ethical considerations, having the DPO involved early on can help avoid potential risks.

- **Example 1: Salesforce and Data Privacy**
  Salesforce's commitment to **data protection** is ingrained in its AI development. By involving the DPO early, the company ensures that ethical considerations like user privacy are prioritized, helping to avoid issues related to **GDPR** compliance.

  - **Impact**: By positioning the DPO as an advisor, Salesforce has successfully navigated several data protection challenges while innovating in AI.

  - **Website**: Salesforce Privacy

- **Example 2: Google and Responsible AI Design**
  Google has made significant strides in AI with a focus on ethical considerations. The company has an established framework for AI development that incorporates **privacy by design** principles, with the DPO serving as a strategic partner during the **design and deployment** phases.

  - **Impact**: Google's focus on responsible AI has not only ensured compliance but has also built public trust.

  - **Website**: Google AI Principles

2. Encouraging Collaboration Between the DPO and AI Teams

Collaboration between the **DPO and AI teams** is essential for building AI systems that are both innovative and ethical. The DPO brings expertise in **data protection**, while AI teams contribute technical knowledge. By working together, they can ensure that data protection is not an afterthought but an integral part of the AI project.

- **Example: IBM Watson and AI Ethics Collaboration**
  IBM Watson collaborates with the DPOs in its AI projects to ensure that its systems meet ethical standards and legal obligations. This partnership leads to more **secure, accountable, and transparent AI models**.

  - **Impact**: The collaboration enhances the quality and trustworthiness of AI outputs while ensuring compliance with data privacy laws.

  - **Website**: IBM Watson AI Ethics

3. Ensuring Ethical and Legal Considerations Are Front-and-Center in AI Design

For AI systems to be truly responsible, **ethical and legal considerations** must be prioritized during the design phase. The DPO's expertise ensures that issues such as data privacy, fairness, and accountability are deeply embedded into the system architecture.

- **Example 1: Accenture's Responsible AI Framework**
  Accenture's **Responsible AI Framework** emphasizes the inclusion of **data ethics** and **compliance** from the beginning of the AI lifecycle. The DPOs at Accenture work closely with AI teams to ensure that **data privacy** and **ethical guidelines** are integrated into every AI project.
  - **Impact**: This proactive approach helps Accenture avoid **data breaches** and ethical dilemmas.
  - **Website**: Accenture Responsible AI

- **Example 2: Microsoft's Ethical AI Design Process**
  Microsoft's approach to ethical AI includes clear guidelines for **data privacy**, **inclusivity**, and **transparency**. The DPO ensures that these considerations are part of every stage of development.
  - **Impact**: Microsoft has gained recognition for its leadership in **ethical AI** and **data protection**, fostering trust and compliance.
  - **Website**: Microsoft AI Ethics

4. Action Point: Work Closely with AI Teams to Embed Data Protection Principles from the Start

- **Step 1: Initiate Early Engagement**: Involve the DPO from the very beginning of AI development, particularly during the design phase, to ensure that data protection principles are incorporated.

- **Step 2: Promote Continuous Collaboration**: Set up regular meetings between the DPO and AI teams throughout the development cycle to monitor compliance and ensure that ethical considerations are consistently integrated.

- **Step 3: Implement Data Protection by Design**: Develop policies and guidelines that ensure every AI project adheres to **privacy by design** principles, making data protection an integral part of the project lifecycle.

Checklist for Embedding Data Protection in AI Projects

Action	Description	Responsible Party	Frequency
Engage DPO Early	Ensure DPO is involved from the project's inception.	AI Team, DPO	At project initiation
Collaborative Meetings	Schedule regular check-ins between the DPO and AI teams.	DPO, AI Team	Monthly
Data Protection by Design	Implement data protection principles throughout the AI lifecycle.	DPO, AI Team	Ongoing
Documentation and Compliance Check	Ensure all AI design decisions are documented for legal compliance.	DPO, Legal Team	Quarterly
Training and Awareness	Educate all team members on AI ethics and data protection.	HR, DPO	Annually

FAQ

Q1: How can the DPO contribute to the AI development process?
A1: The DPO can act as a trusted advisor, ensuring that data protection and ethical considerations are integrated from the very beginning of the AI lifecycle, helping to mitigate risks and ensure compliance with data privacy laws.

Q2: What is the importance of collaboration between the DPO and AI teams?
A2: Collaboration ensures that ethical and legal standards are consistently applied throughout the development process, resulting in more responsible, transparent, and compliant AI systems.

Q3: How can AI teams ensure they are addressing ethical considerations from the start?
A3: AI teams should work closely with the DPO to embed **data protection principles** such as **privacy by design** and **transparency** into the development process, ensuring the system complies with legal and ethical standards.

MOTD

"AI innovation is best when built on a foundation of ethical principles; let the DPO guide the way."

Chapter 9: DPOs and AI Data Ethics in Practice
9.5 Establishing a DPO-Led AI Ethics Framework

1. Developing a Clear Ethical Framework for AI Development and Deployment

To ensure AI systems are developed and deployed in an ethical manner, it is crucial to establish a **clear ethical framework**. This framework should outline the guiding principles, practices, and policies related to **data protection**, **privacy**, **transparency**, and **accountability**. The DPO plays a pivotal role in shaping these principles by providing expert guidance on data ethics and ensuring that AI systems adhere to both legal and ethical standards.

- **Example 1**: **Google AI Principles**
  Google developed a set of AI principles to guide the ethical development of its AI technologies. The DPO, in collaboration with AI teams, ensured that these principles were embedded into the AI development process. The principles focus on fairness, transparency, and avoiding harm to individuals.

  - **Impact**: This approach has helped Google navigate complex ethical concerns in AI and build public trust.

  - **Website**: Google AI Principles

- **Example 2**: **IBM's Ethical AI Framework**
  IBM created an AI ethics framework that emphasizes transparency, fairness, and accountability in AI decision-making. The DPO is responsible for ensuring compliance with this framework and for working with AI teams to ensure ethical considerations are consistently applied.

  - **Impact**: This framework ensures that AI systems built by IBM remain ethical and legally compliant.

  - **Website**: IBM AI Ethics

2. Best Practices for Creating and Implementing an AI Ethics Policy

When creating and implementing an AI ethics policy, best practices include:

- **Incorporating AI Ethics Early in Development**: Involve the DPO from the earliest stages of AI system design to ensure that ethical considerations are part of the development process.

- **Stakeholder Engagement**: Consult with a range of stakeholders—including legal teams, business leaders, and external experts—when developing the policy to ensure a comprehensive, diverse perspective.

- **Clear Guidelines for AI Development**: Develop clear guidelines on data collection, data usage, fairness, transparency, and accountability.

- **Ongoing Training and Awareness**: Regularly train all employees, including AI developers, on AI ethics and data protection standards.

- **Example 1: Microsoft Responsible AI Standard**
  Microsoft's Responsible AI Standard is a robust policy developed to promote fairness, transparency, and accountability in AI systems. The DPO ensures that every AI system complies with these standards and is regularly reviewed for ethical concerns.

  - **Impact**: The DPO's oversight has helped Microsoft build AI that is both innovative and ethically responsible.

  - **Website**: Microsoft Responsible AI

- **Example 2: Accenture AI Ethics Framework**
  Accenture has developed an AI Ethics Framework that includes guidelines on the **ethical use of AI**, **privacy**, and **transparency**. The DPO is responsible for ensuring that these policies are followed in every AI project.

  - **Impact**: The framework ensures that Accenture's AI initiatives are not only innovative but also adhere to high ethical standards.

  - **Website**: Accenture Responsible AI

3. The DPO's Responsibility for Oversight and Continuous Monitoring of AI Systems

Once the ethical framework and policies are in place, it is the DPO's responsibility to provide **continuous oversight** of AI systems. This includes:

- **Monitoring AI Systems Post-Deployment**: Continuously monitor deployed AI systems for any signs of **bias**, **inaccuracy**, or **unethical behavior**.

- **Auditing AI Decisions**: Conduct periodic audits of AI systems to ensure they are making ethical decisions in line with the established framework.

- **Feedback Loops**: Create feedback loops that allow for **real-time monitoring** and improvement of AI systems based on ethical principles.

- **Example: The European Commission's AI Guidelines**
  The European Commission has established guidelines to ensure that AI systems adhere to ethical principles. DPOs are critical in ensuring that AI development within the EU remains compliant with these standards, ensuring that AI is used responsibly and ethically.

  - **Impact**: This continuous monitoring helps prevent bias and ensures that AI systems serve societal needs ethically and responsibly.

  - **Website**: European Commission AI Guidelines

4. Action Point: Create and Regularly Review an AI Ethics Framework Within Your Organization

- **Step 1**: **Define Ethical Guidelines**: Start by clearly defining ethical guidelines for AI development that cover **data privacy**, **transparency**, and **accountability**.

- **Step 2**: **Incorporate DPO Expertise**: Involve the DPO in the creation and continuous revision of the ethical guidelines to ensure they align with both legal requirements and ethical best practices.

- **Step 3**: **Conduct Regular Reviews**: Regularly review and update the framework to address new ethical challenges, ensure compliance, and improve the organization's AI practices.

Checklist for Establishing an AI Ethics Framework

Action	Description	Responsible Party	Frequency
Create Ethical Guidelines	Develop clear ethical standards for AI development.	DPO, AI Team	One-time
Engage Stakeholders	Consult with legal, business, and ethical experts.	DPO, Legal Team, Business	One-time
Continuous Monitoring	Implement ongoing monitoring for AI systems post-deployment.	DPO, AI Team	Ongoing
Periodic Audits	Schedule regular audits to assess AI system compliance.	DPO, AI Team	Quarterly
Training & Awareness	Provide continuous training on AI ethics and data protection.	HR, DPO	Annually

---

FAQ

Q1: Why is it important for the DPO to lead the AI ethics framework?
A1: The DPO ensures that data protection and ethical considerations are embedded into AI systems from the start, mitigating risks related to privacy violations and ensuring compliance with legal standards.

Q2: How can AI teams integrate ethics into the development process?
A2: By collaborating with the DPO to establish clear ethical guidelines, conduct regular audits, and engage stakeholders, AI teams can ensure that ethical considerations are central to the development and deployment of AI systems.

Q3: What role does the DPO play in post-deployment AI monitoring?
A3: The DPO is responsible for continuous oversight of AI systems, ensuring they adhere to ethical standards, identifying any ethical issues that arise, and implementing corrective actions as necessary.

MOTD

"Ethical AI is not a destination, but a continuous journey—let your DPO be the guide."

Chapter 10: The Future of AI and Data Protection

10.1 Trends in AI Development and Data Protection

1. Emerging AI Technologies and Their Data Protection Implications

As AI technologies evolve, so do the data protection challenges. Some emerging AI technologies that are creating both opportunities and challenges for data protection include:

- **AI-Powered Predictive Analytics**: AI systems now utilize vast amounts of personal data to make predictions about consumer behavior, health conditions, or financial risk. This raises concerns about the accuracy of predictions and potential misuse of sensitive data.

- **Generative AI**: With advancements in generative AI, systems like **GPT-3** and **DALL·E** are generating content based on user input. The ability of AI to create personal or potentially sensitive content opens up new concerns about data ownership and privacy violations.

- **Edge Computing and AI**: With the increase in edge computing, AI systems can process data locally on devices rather than sending it to centralized cloud servers. While this reduces data transfer risks, it creates new challenges in securing data on individual devices.

Example 1: AI-Powered Healthcare Systems
AI in healthcare is being used to predict diseases or identify early health risks. While this can vastly improve medical outcomes, it also raises concerns about sensitive health data being misused or exposed.

- **Impact**: This has sparked a need for robust data protection laws and transparent AI practices to ensure that patients' data is not exploited.

- **Website**: AI in Healthcare

Example 2: AI and Financial Institutions
AI-powered systems in financial institutions predict loan approval, detect fraud, and assess creditworthiness. The use of personal data in these systems heightens concerns about **bias** and **discrimination**, especially when decisions are made without human intervention.

- **Impact**: Financial institutions are increasingly adopting AI ethics guidelines to prevent discriminatory practices.

- **Website**: AI in Financial Sector

2. The Shift Toward More Regulated AI Development

Governments and regulators are waking up to the need for comprehensive AI regulations. In particular, the **EU AI Act** is pushing forward a regulatory framework for AI that is grounded in safety and ethics. Similar initiatives are emerging globally, focusing on AI transparency, accountability, and data protection.

Some key aspects of these evolving regulations include:

- **Risk-Based Approach**: Regulations focus on **high-risk AI systems** that may significantly impact individuals or society, such as facial recognition or healthcare AI.

- **AI Audits**: Future regulations may require regular audits of AI systems to ensure they are compliant with data protection laws like GDPR.

- **Data Minimization**: New guidelines may demand that only necessary data be used for AI operations, ensuring that individuals' privacy is prioritized.

Example: EU AI Act
The European Union is advancing the **AI Act**, which will regulate AI development and use. It emphasizes transparency, accountability, and respect for privacy and data protection.

- **Impact**: This will require AI developers to rethink their systems, ensuring they can meet the stringent standards imposed by this Act.

- **Website**: EU AI Act

3. Predictions for the Future of AI in Data Privacy and Protection

In the next 5-10 years, we can expect several key trends in the intersection of AI and data privacy:

- **Increased Use of Privacy-Preserving AI**: AI systems will increasingly adopt techniques like **federated learning** or **differential privacy**, which enable AI to learn from data without accessing personal information.

- **Stronger Regulations**: The global push for stronger AI regulations will likely lead to more comprehensive, standardized frameworks for AI development, including clear guidelines on data privacy.

- **AI for Cybersecurity**: AI will become a key tool in defending against data breaches, with AI systems able to predict and detect vulnerabilities in real time.

Example: Privacy-Preserving AI at Apple
Apple's use of **differential privacy** in its iOS devices helps ensure that the data collected is anonymized, preventing any personal data from being exposed.

- **Impact**: Privacy-preserving AI methods will play a key role in ensuring that AI systems respect privacy while still delivering valuable insights.

- **Website**: Apple Privacy

Action Point: Stay Ahead of Emerging Trends in AI and Data Protection

To stay ahead in this rapidly evolving space:

1. **Follow Regulatory Developments**: Regularly monitor AI regulations in your region (such as the **EU AI Act** or local data protection laws).

2. **Implement Privacy-Preserving Technologies**: Adopt techniques like **federated learning** and **differential privacy** to ensure your AI systems respect users' privacy.

3. **Collaborate with Experts**: Work with legal, technical, and data protection experts to ensure that your AI systems are fully compliant with data protection laws.

Checklist for Staying Ahead in AI Data Protection

Action	Description	Responsible Party	Frequency
Monitor Regulatory Changes	Stay updated on new AI regulations and compliance requirements.	DPO, Legal Team	Monthly
Adopt Privacy-Preserving AI Techniques	Implement federated learning or differential privacy.	AI, Data Protection Team	Quarterly
Collaborate with Experts	Engage with AI, legal, and ethical experts for cross-department collaboration.	DPO, AI, Legal	Ongoing
Regular AI System Audits	Conduct AI system audits to ensure compliance with privacy and ethical standards.	DPO, AI Team	Annually

---

FAQ

Q1: What is the EU AI Act, and how does it impact AI development?
A1: The **EU AI Act** is a regulatory framework that will guide the ethical development of AI in the European Union. It imposes strict guidelines on high-risk AI applications to ensure they align with data protection, transparency, and accountability standards.

Q2: How does privacy-preserving AI work?
A2: Privacy-preserving AI techniques like **federated learning** and **differential privacy** enable AI systems to learn from data without accessing or storing sensitive personal information, helping to protect user privacy.

Q3: How can companies stay ahead of emerging AI and data protection trends?
A3: Companies can stay ahead by monitoring regulatory changes, adopting privacy-preserving technologies, and collaborating with experts to ensure their AI systems are both innovative and compliant with data protection standards.

MOTD

"AI's future is bright, but it's our responsibility to ensure that it's built with privacy, ethics, and transparency at its core."

Chapter 10: The Future of AI and Data Protection
10.2 The Evolving Role of the DPO in the AI Era

1. How the Role of the DPO Will Evolve as AI Continues to Grow

As AI technologies become more integral to business operations, the role of the **Data Protection Officer (DPO)** will need to evolve. In the AI era, the DPO's responsibilities will extend beyond traditional data privacy oversight to include **AI ethics**, **algorithmic accountability**, and **AI governance**.

Key changes in the DPO role include:

- **Oversight of AI-Driven Data Collection**: AI systems require vast amounts of data, often personal in nature. The DPO must ensure that these data collection processes are transparent, lawful, and aligned with privacy regulations.

- **Monitoring AI Decision-Making**: As AI begins making autonomous decisions in areas like credit scoring, healthcare diagnosis, and recruitment, the DPO will need to ensure that these systems operate in a way that's fair, non-discriminatory, and compliant with data protection laws.

Example 1: AI in Healthcare AI is transforming healthcare by analyzing medical data to make predictions about patient outcomes. A DPO in a healthcare organization would ensure that AI systems comply with strict **HIPAA** (Health Insurance Portability and Accountability Act) regulations, protecting patient data while leveraging AI to improve health outcomes.

- **Impact**: The DPO ensures patient privacy is respected while AI improves diagnostic accuracy.

- **Website**: AI in Healthcare

Example 2: AI in Recruitment Companies using AI to screen job candidates must ensure that algorithms do not perpetuate biases. The DPO will oversee how personal data is processed by these AI systems and ensure compliance with **GDPR** and **EEOC** (Equal Employment Opportunity Commission) regulations.

- **Impact**: By guiding AI systems towards fairness, the DPO helps avoid discrimination in hiring practices.

- **Website**: AI in Recruitment

2. Adapting to New AI-Related Regulations and Guidelines

As AI technologies grow, so will the regulatory frameworks surrounding them. The DPO will need to stay on top of evolving laws, such as the **EU AI Act**, which imposes specific requirements on high-risk AI systems. They must also be prepared for new regulations that could affect data privacy and AI ethics.

- **Regulatory Updates**: The DPO will need to monitor the latest developments in AI law, ensuring the organization stays compliant with both **GDPR** and emerging AI regulations globally.

- **Risk-Based Approach**: With the introduction of the EU AI Act and similar legislation, DPOs will have to adopt a **risk-based approach** to compliance, identifying and mitigating risks associated with high-risk AI applications.

Example: EU AI Act The **EU AI Act** introduces regulations for AI systems based on their risk level. DPOs in European companies must ensure that high-risk AI systems are transparent and accountable, particularly when processing personal data.

- **Impact**: This requires DPOs to constantly assess the organization's AI practices, ensuring they align with new legal requirements.

- **Website**: EU AI Act Overview

3. Becoming a Key Player in AI Ethics and Development Teams

As AI continues to evolve, DPOs will need to be integral to AI development teams. They will help ensure that **data protection** and **AI ethics** are incorporated into AI products from the start—what is known as "privacy by design."

- **AI Ethics Integration**: The DPO will need to ensure that ethical considerations, such as fairness, transparency, and non-discrimination, are part of AI system development.

- **Collaboration with AI Teams**: DPOs will increasingly collaborate with engineers, data scientists, and legal teams to assess AI models for compliance with data protection laws and ethical guidelines.

Example: AI Ethics in Autonomous Vehicles For autonomous vehicle companies, DPOs will collaborate with AI engineers to ensure that data from vehicle sensors is collected, stored, and processed in a way that respects privacy and adheres to regulatory requirements, such as **GDPR**.

- **Impact**: Ensuring that AI systems in autonomous vehicles operate ethically and legally enhances public trust and minimizes legal risk.

- **Website**: Autonomous Vehicle AI Ethics

Action Point: Position Yourself as a Future-Ready DPO for AI-Driven Organizations

To prepare for the future of AI and data protection:

1. **Stay Informed on Emerging Regulations**: Regularly track global AI legislation and guidelines, such as the **EU AI Act** and other regional laws.

2. **Engage with AI Development Teams**: Build relationships with AI engineers and data scientists to embed data protection and ethics early in the development process.

3. **Adopt a Risk-Based Approach**: Implement a risk-based approach to assess AI systems' potential impact on privacy and ensure that high-risk AI systems are fully compliant with regulations.

Checklist for a Future-Ready DPO in AI-Driven Organizations

Action	Description	Responsible Party	Frequency
Track AI Regulatory Developments	Stay informed about new AI-related laws and regulations.	DPO, Legal Team	Monthly
Engage in AI Ethics Discussions	Regularly collaborate with AI teams to address ethical considerations.	DPO, AI Team	Ongoing
Conduct AI Risk Assessments	Evaluate and mitigate risks associated with AI systems.	DPO, Risk Team	Quarterly
Implement Privacy by Design	Ensure that AI systems are designed with data protection in mind.	DPO, AI Team	Ongoing

FAQ

Q1: What does "privacy by design" mean in the context of AI development?
A1: "Privacy by design" refers to the practice of integrating privacy protections into the development of AI systems from the outset, ensuring that data privacy is maintained throughout the lifecycle of the technology.

Q2: How can a DPO help with AI ethics?
A2: A DPO can ensure that AI systems are developed and deployed in compliance with ethical standards, such as fairness, transparency, and non-discrimination, while also making sure that personal data is protected.

Q3: Why is the DPO role becoming more important in AI development?
A3: As AI systems handle vast amounts of sensitive data and make autonomous decisions, the DPO's role is crucial in ensuring that these systems comply with privacy laws and ethical standards, minimizing risks for both individuals and organizations.

MOTD

"Embrace change, stay ahead, and be the guardian of ethical AI in tomorrow's world."

Chapter 10: The Future of AI and Data Protection

10.3 Preparing for the Challenges of Tomorrow

As AI continues to evolve, so do the challenges surrounding data protection and ethical use. Preparing for the future involves anticipating changes, future-proofing strategies, and staying ahead of regulatory updates. Here's how to prepare for the future of AI in data protection:

---

1. Anticipating Future Challenges in AI and Data Protection
AI technologies, particularly deep learning, machine learning, and natural language processing, bring unique challenges for data privacy. The increasing complexity and data volume raise concerns around the collection, storage, and processing of personal data. Future challenges include the potential for AI to be used in harmful ways, such as deepfakes or surveillance, or increased risks due to data breaches. Organizations must stay ahead by continuously monitoring advancements in AI and the evolving data protection landscape.

- **Example:** The deployment of facial recognition AI in public spaces could result in mass surveillance and privacy violations. In response, companies like IBM have ceased offering facial recognition technology in response to privacy concerns and potential regulatory pressure (Source: IBM).

- **Impact:** Ensuring ethical considerations in AI deployment is crucial to avoid risks like misuse of data and unintended bias, which can negatively affect user trust and regulatory compliance.

---

2. How to Future-Proof Your AI Data Ethics Strategies
Future-proofing AI data ethics requires integrating privacy-by-design and accountability into AI systems from the outset. This includes aligning with GDPR and other global standards, and ensuring that AI algorithms are transparent and explainable. A proactive strategy includes embedding ethical reviews at every stage of the AI development lifecycle and adopting a culture of continuous improvement.

- **Example:** Google's AI Principles aim to ensure their AI technologies are developed in a responsible way, particularly regarding privacy, fairness, and transparency. They emphasize transparency in AI decision-making and have incorporated feedback mechanisms from external experts (Source: Google AI).

- **Impact:** Google's commitment to ethics helps mitigate risks and builds trust with users by addressing potential issues before they arise, fostering greater transparency.

3. The Evolving Relationship Between AI, Ethics, and Regulation

As AI adoption grows, so will the regulatory environment around its use. Governments and international bodies are increasingly developing regulations aimed at ensuring responsible AI. The evolving relationship between AI, ethics, and regulation will demand organizations to adapt quickly to legal changes while maintaining high ethical standards. For example, the EU is working on the **Artificial Intelligence Act** to regulate AI deployment based on the level of risk. Staying informed and aligning with these regulations will be crucial for compliance.

- **Example:** The **GDPR** has already set the tone for data protection laws, and the upcoming EU AI regulation seeks to impose stricter requirements on high-risk AI applications (Source: European Commission).

- **Impact:** Companies aligning early with these regulations can avoid hefty fines and improve public perception by showing their commitment to responsible AI practices.

Action Point:

Start preparing today for tomorrow's AI challenges. Regularly review and update your AI ethics strategies, ensure compliance with emerging laws, and foster a culture of ethical AI development within your organization. Position yourself and your team as leaders in responsible AI deployment.

FAQ

Q1: How can I anticipate future challenges in AI and data protection?
A1: Regularly engage with the latest AI trends, participate in industry forums, and closely monitor regulatory changes. Collaborating with AI teams and legal experts can help you foresee potential risks before they become significant problems.

Q2: What steps should we take to future-proof our AI data ethics strategy?
A2: Implement privacy-by-design principles, engage in continuous training and ethical reviews, and align with emerging regulations such as GDPR and the upcoming EU AI Act. It's essential to create a roadmap that integrates privacy and ethical considerations from the start of AI development.

Q3: How do emerging AI regulations affect my current data protection policies?
A3: Emerging regulations will likely bring stricter compliance requirements. Regular audits and updates to your current policies will ensure they align with these changes. Engage with legal teams to ensure your systems meet the evolving regulatory standards.

MOTD (Message of the Day)

"Staying ahead of the curve today ensures a secure, ethical tomorrow for AI."

Chapter 10: The Future of AI and Data Protection

10.4 The Global Perspective: AI and Data Protection Around the World

In today's interconnected world, the role of data protection in AI development is influenced by regulations, case studies, and international cooperation. As AI technologies become increasingly global, understanding the diverse regulatory landscapes is crucial for organizations to stay compliant and build trust with users.

---

1. Global Regulations and Their Impact on AI Data Protection

AI and data protection regulations vary widely across regions, and organizations must comply with multiple frameworks depending on their geographical reach. The **General Data Protection Regulation (GDPR)** in the EU, for instance, sets stringent guidelines on data processing and privacy, significantly affecting AI systems that deal with personal data. Similarly, the **California Consumer Privacy Act (CCPA)** in the United States influences how businesses manage consumer data, particularly for AI-driven applications that rely on large datasets.

- **Example:** In 2021, **Amazon's Ring** faced scrutiny in California for failing to notify users about the sharing of their personal data with law enforcement without consent, highlighting the need for better data protection and transparency under CCPA and GDPR standards (Source: TechCrunch).

- **Impact:** Non-compliance with these regulations can result in severe financial penalties, damage to reputation, and erosion of consumer trust. Staying ahead of regulatory changes is key to mitigating these risks.

---

2. Case Studies from Different Regions on AI and Data Privacy

Different regions have taken varied approaches to AI data protection. In Europe, the EU's **GDPR** provides a robust framework, while China has implemented the **Personal Information Protection Law (PIPL)**, which imposes strict controls on the collection and use of personal data, particularly by AI companies. Meanwhile, the United States has a more fragmented approach with state-level laws like **CCPA**, and pending federal legislation on AI governance.

- **Example:** China's **PIPL** law imposes severe penalties on companies that breach privacy provisions, particularly those using AI for facial recognition. This legislation has forced companies like **Alibaba** and **Tencent** to overhaul their data practices to ensure compliance (Source: South China Morning Post).

- **Impact:** These global regulations provide different challenges and opportunities for AI companies. While Europe focuses on consumer rights, China emphasizes strict control over data usage. Organizations must adapt their strategies to comply with the local laws in each region where they operate.

---

3. The Role of International Cooperation in AI Governance

International cooperation is vital in AI governance, as AI technologies cross borders and can impact privacy globally. Collaborative efforts, like the **OECD AI Principles**, help set common guidelines for responsible AI development and data protection. These principles aim to promote transparency, fairness, and accountability, ensuring that AI systems respect privacy rights and operate in the public interest.

- **Example:** The **OECD AI Principles**, adopted by over 40 countries, aim to provide consistent governance on AI, ensuring ethical AI development while balancing innovation and privacy protection (Source: OECD).

- **Impact:** These international efforts foster alignment on AI standards, helping businesses navigate global regulations and ensuring AI technologies are developed in a socially responsible manner.

Action Point:

Stay informed about the global regulatory landscape surrounding AI and data protection. Monitor changes in key regions such as the EU, China, and the U.S., and ensure your organization is prepared to comply with evolving international standards.

FAQ

Q1: How do global regulations impact AI data protection?
A1: Global regulations, like GDPR in Europe and PIPL in China, impose varying requirements on how personal data can be collected, used, and processed by AI systems. Non-compliance can result in heavy fines and reputational damage, so businesses must understand the legal frameworks in every region where they operate.

Q2: What role does international cooperation play in AI governance?
A2: International cooperation helps align AI governance principles across countries, creating a shared understanding of ethical AI practices. Initiatives like the OECD AI Principles promote fairness, transparency, and accountability, which help standardize AI development and data protection efforts worldwide.

Q3: How can I keep track of global AI regulations?
A3: Regularly monitor updates from key regulatory bodies, subscribe to legal newsletters, and engage with industry forums focused on AI and data protection.

Developing a global compliance strategy will ensure your organization stays up to date with evolving laws.

MOTD (Message of the Day)

"Embrace global compliance to ensure responsible AI innovation and safeguard user trust."

Chapter 10: The Future of AI and Data Protection

10.5 The DPO's Role in Shaping the Future of AI

The Data Protection Officer (DPO) is more than just a compliance gatekeeper —
they are key leaders in shaping the ethical trajectory of AI technologies. As AI
continues to evolve, the DPO plays a pivotal role in ensuring that AI systems respect
privacy, promote fairness, and foster accountability. Here's how DPOs can take on
leadership roles in AI ethics and governance.

---

1. Leadership Opportunities for DPOs in AI Ethics and Governance

DPOs are uniquely positioned to drive AI ethics within organizations. As AI systems
become more integral to business operations, DPOs can lead the charge in shaping
policies that align with ethical principles, transparency, and compliance. The
leadership role includes advising executive teams, crafting AI ethics strategies, and
ensuring these strategies align with both legal standards and societal expectations.

- **Example: Microsoft's AI and Ethics Committee** includes their Chief Privacy
  Officer (CPO), who also serves as a strategic advisor on data protection and
  AI ethics. This allows the CPO (and DPO) to influence the company's stance
  on privacy rights in AI products. Microsoft's AI policy emphasizes fairness,
  inclusivity, and transparency, setting a high bar for AI ethics (Source:
  Microsoft AI Principles).

- **Impact:** By placing the DPO in a leadership role, organizations integrate
  ethical considerations into every aspect of AI development. This leadership
  enhances trust among consumers and stakeholders, paving the way for
  responsible AI deployment.

---

2. How DPOs Can Influence AI Industry Standards and Best Practices

DPOs can contribute to shaping broader industry standards for AI. By participating in
industry groups, forums, and policy discussions, DPOs can help draft guidelines and
standards that reflect responsible data handling practices. Their input ensures that AI
developers integrate privacy and ethics into the core of their designs.

- **Example:** The **European Commission** has relied on the expertise of DPOs
  and data protection professionals in creating the **Ethics Guidelines for
  Trustworthy AI**, which outline key principles for ethical AI development.
  DPOs play a crucial role in providing input to ensure these guidelines align
  with data protection principles.

- **Impact:** Influencing such standards not only enhances the ethical foundation of AI but also allows companies to proactively adapt to future regulatory changes, ensuring they remain at the forefront of the ethical AI movement.

3. Building a Legacy of Ethical AI in Your Organization

DPOs can create a lasting impact by embedding ethical AI practices into the organization's DNA. This involves creating an AI ethics framework that is sustainable and evolves with technology. By establishing clear ethical guidelines and embedding them into AI development cycles, DPOs build a legacy of responsible AI that will benefit both the organization and society at large.

- **Example: IBM's Watson AI** has implemented an ethical framework around its AI system, where the DPO helps lead the efforts to ensure privacy and fairness. This proactive approach has resulted in clear ethical guidelines that not only guide internal development but also influence industry-wide practices (Source: IBM Watson AI Ethics).

- **Impact:** A DPO-driven ethical AI framework can create a long-term culture of responsible AI development. It strengthens an organization's reputation as a leader in ethical AI and promotes public trust in its products and services.

Action Point:

Take an active role in shaping the future of ethical AI within your organization. Start by embedding data protection principles into AI strategies and work closely with AI teams to ensure that ethics, privacy, and transparency are prioritized at every stage of AI development.

FAQ

Q1: How can DPOs influence AI industry standards?
A1: DPOs can contribute to AI industry standards by participating in regulatory discussions, offering insights on data protection, and helping draft policies that balance innovation with ethical considerations. Their expertise ensures that industry standards align with privacy laws and ethical principles.

Q2: What leadership opportunities exist for DPOs in AI ethics?
A2: DPOs can take on leadership roles by advising executive teams on AI ethics, leading AI ethics committees, and driving the integration of privacy principles into AI system designs. This positions them as strategic leaders in shaping the ethical direction of AI technologies.

Q3: How can DPOs build a legacy of ethical AI in their organizations?
A3: DPOs can build a legacy by developing and implementing an AI ethics framework that incorporates privacy, fairness, and transparency. By integrating these practices into the organization's culture, DPOs ensure long-term ethical AI development and positive public perception.

MOTD (Message of the Day)

"Lead with ethics, innovate with integrity — that's how DPOs shape the future of AI."

Chapter 11: Conclusion and Key Takeaways

11.1 Recap of the DPO's Responsibilities in AI Ethics

As we conclude this book, it's essential to reflect on the critical role Data Protection Officers (DPOs) play in ensuring the ethical development and deployment of AI systems. DPOs are pivotal in balancing the drive for innovation with the need for data protection, privacy, and accountability.

---

1. Summary of Key Insights from the Book

Throughout this book, we've emphasized how DPOs can steer organizations towards responsible AI use while ensuring compliance with data protection laws. Key themes include:

- **The importance of ethical AI**: DPOs are tasked with ensuring AI systems align with both legal and moral standards.

- **Data protection and AI**: AI development requires close monitoring to avoid misuse of personal data and ensure transparency in algorithms.

- **Strategic role of the DPO**: DPOs must not just enforce data protection laws but also act as strategic advisors in the ethical deployment of AI systems.

By positioning themselves at the intersection of AI innovation and legal compliance, DPOs are not just regulators but leaders shaping the future of AI ethics.

---

2. Core Functions of a DPO in AI and Data Protection

The core responsibilities of a DPO in the AI era are multifaceted. They include:

- **Compliance Monitoring**: DPOs ensure AI systems comply with data protection laws (e.g., GDPR, CCPA) and internal policies.

- **Risk Management**: DPOs identify and mitigate risks related to AI data processing and security breaches.

- **Ethical Oversight**: DPOs advocate for the integration of ethical principles, such as fairness and accountability, into AI development.

- **Collaboration with AI teams**: DPOs work closely with AI development teams to ensure ethical design, from data collection to algorithmic transparency.

---

3. The Importance of Ethical AI Practices for Privacy and Accountability

Ethical AI practices are essential for ensuring that AI systems respect user privacy and operate transparently. As AI technologies grow more complex, their ability to process vast amounts of personal data increases, raising the potential for misuse or discriminatory outcomes. DPOs are at the forefront of advocating for privacy and ethical standards within AI systems. By embedding data protection principles early in AI development, DPOs help mitigate legal, reputational, and financial risks.

Example 1: **Google DeepMind** has been proactive in ensuring ethical AI practices by setting up a specific Ethics & Society team. The team ensures that AI technologies, particularly those in healthcare, respect privacy and are transparent about how data is used (Source: DeepMind Health Ethics).

Impact: DeepMind's approach to integrating ethical oversight into AI development builds trust with users and stakeholders while ensuring compliance with data protection laws.

Example 2: **Salesforce** has invested in creating an AI ethics board that evaluates the company's AI technologies, ensuring they meet privacy standards and ethical guidelines (Source: Salesforce AI Ethics).

Impact: Salesforce's ethics board enables the company to adopt a proactive approach to ethical concerns and reinforces its commitment to using AI in a responsible, transparent way.

Action Point: Reflect on Your Role and Plan for Proactive Steps in Advocating Ethical AI Systems

As a DPO, it's essential to take a step back and evaluate your role within the organization, especially regarding AI ethics. Consider the following:

- **Reflect**: Are you actively participating in AI development discussions? Are data protection principles considered at the early stages of AI projects?

- **Plan**: Develop a strategy for embedding ethical AI practices within your organization. This could involve creating new frameworks, training AI teams, or collaborating with external experts to stay ahead of industry standards.

Taking a proactive approach ensures that your organization not only complies with laws but also leads the way in ethical AI development.

FAQ

Q1: What is the DPO's role in ensuring ethical AI development?
A1: The DPO ensures that AI systems comply with data protection regulations and

ethical standards. They collaborate with AI teams to integrate privacy, fairness, and transparency into AI design, minimizing risks such as bias and misuse of personal data.

Q2: How can a DPO advocate for ethical AI in their organization?
A2: A DPO can advocate by creating frameworks that promote transparency, fairness, and accountability in AI systems. They can also work with AI developers to embed these values into AI models from the start, ensuring privacy rights are respected.

Q3: Why is it essential to focus on ethical AI practices?
A3: Ethical AI practices are critical for ensuring that AI systems operate in ways that are fair, transparent, and respect individual privacy. This helps organizations build trust with their users, avoid regulatory fines, and prevent harmful outcomes.

MOTD (Message of the Day)

"Ethical AI isn't just a guideline—it's a responsibility. Lead the change by embedding data protection and fairness at the core of AI development."

Chapter 11: Conclusion and Key Takeaways

11.2 Essential Tools and Mindsets for Success

To ensure success in managing AI-related data protection, DPOs must have access to the right tools and adopt the right mindsets. The tools help streamline compliance, monitoring, and risk management, while the mindsets help DPOs lead ethically and proactively in the ever-evolving landscape of AI and data protection.

---

1. Key Tools DPOs Need to Manage AI-Related Data Protection

As AI systems become more complex, DPOs need robust tools to ensure compliance with data protection laws and ethical standards. Some essential tools include:

- **Audit Frameworks**: These frameworks help track and document the processes involved in AI data usage. They are crucial for assessing the transparency and accountability of AI models. Regular audits also enable the identification of potential risks such as data bias, data breaches, and non-compliance with privacy laws.

- **Risk Assessment Tools**: DPOs need to use risk assessment tools like **Data Protection Impact Assessments (DPIAs)** or **Automated Risk Management Platforms** to evaluate the potential risks posed by AI systems. These tools help ensure that risks such as data misuse, bias in algorithms, and privacy violations are identified and mitigated early in the design phase.

- **Privacy Management Software**: Solutions like OneTrust and TrustArc provide comprehensive privacy compliance frameworks, allowing DPOs to manage data protection laws across various jurisdictions and sectors. These tools can automate compliance checks and provide reporting for audits.

Example 1: **OneTrust** helps companies manage privacy risks across AI initiatives by offering tools to perform DPIAs, track consent, and manage data retention. OneTrust is used by companies like **Nestlé** and **Cisco** to streamline data protection processes and ensure regulatory compliance.
Website URL

Impact: With OneTrust, organizations reduce their risk of violating data protection laws, making it easier to scale AI projects with compliance.

---

2. Necessary Mindsets: Proactive Compliance, Ethical Leadership, and Collaboration

- **Proactive Compliance**: A DPO must be forward-thinking, anticipating challenges before they arise. This involves understanding future regulations, anticipating potential risks, and making compliance an ongoing process rather than a one-time event. For example, DPOs can stay ahead by attending conferences and subscribing to regulatory updates about AI and data privacy.

- **Ethical Leadership**: The DPO should take on the role of an ethical leader, advocating for fairness, transparency, and accountability in AI systems. They must act as a moral compass within the organization, ensuring AI applications are designed with ethical principles in mind.

- **Collaboration**: DPOs must collaborate not only with IT and legal teams but also with AI developers and data scientists. AI ethics requires a multidisciplinary approach where the DPO's expertise is integrated early in the development phase.

Example 2: **IBM** integrates ethical leadership into its AI development by establishing a set of AI principles. Their **AI Ethics Board** helps guide the ethical deployment of AI and offers a model for other organizations to follow.
Website URL

Impact: IBM's proactive approach to AI ethics helps to build trust with customers, regulators, and other stakeholders. Their AI principles ensure that their AI solutions are developed with integrity, which leads to better market reception and fewer ethical controversies.

Action Point: Familiarize Yourself with the Right Tools and Mindsets for AI Data Protection Success

To be successful in the AI data protection space, familiarize yourself with the tools and mindsets that will help you navigate the complexities of AI regulation and ethics. Start by investing in risk management tools, privacy management software, and audit frameworks. Equally important is adopting a proactive compliance mindset, leading with ethics, and fostering collaboration with AI teams.

FAQ

Q1: What are some critical tools that DPOs should use to manage AI data protection?
A1: DPOs should utilize audit frameworks, risk assessment tools, and privacy management software to ensure that AI systems comply with data protection laws and are ethically designed. Tools like OneTrust and TrustArc help automate compliance checks and conduct Data Protection Impact Assessments (DPIAs).

Q2: How can DPOs lead ethically in AI data protection?
A2: DPOs can lead ethically by advocating for transparency, fairness, and accountability in AI systems. They should ensure that ethical principles are

integrated from the start of AI development and collaborate closely with AI teams to mitigate risks such as algorithmic bias or data misuse.

Q3: Why is collaboration important for DPOs working with AI teams?
A3: Collaboration ensures that data protection principles are embedded early in the AI development process. By working with AI developers, legal teams, and other stakeholders, DPOs can help ensure that AI systems are compliant and ethically designed.

MOTD (Message of the Day)

"Equip yourself with the right tools, adopt the right mindset, and be the champion of ethical AI in your organization."

Chapter 11: Conclusion and Key Takeaways

11.3 A Call to Action: Leading the Charge in Ethical AI Protection

As artificial intelligence (AI) continues to reshape industries, the responsibility of Data Protection Officers (DPOs) is more important than ever. In the age of AI, DPOs must not only ensure legal compliance but also advocate for ethical practices that protect individuals' privacy, promote fairness, and foster trust in AI technologies. This call to action emphasizes the growing leadership role of DPOs in ethical AI governance and offers actionable steps to lead the charge in promoting responsible AI use within organizations.

---

1. The Growing Role of DPOs in Ethical AI Governance

As AI technologies become increasingly prevalent, the role of the DPO expands beyond traditional data protection tasks. DPOs must take on an active role in AI governance, ensuring that AI systems are designed, deployed, and monitored in ways that respect privacy, fairness, and transparency. DPOs need to collaborate with cross-functional teams to provide guidance on ethical issues and to make sure that AI systems align with both legal requirements and ethical standards.

- **Example: Google's AI Principles**: Google has established clear principles around AI ethics, emphasizing fairness, accountability, and transparency. The DPO or data privacy teams at companies like Google can influence the ethical direction of AI projects, ensuring alignment with organizational values. Website URL

Impact: Google's principles help mitigate the risk of bias and unfair outcomes, which can occur if AI systems are poorly managed, and ensure the company is seen as a leader in ethical AI practices.

---

2. Becoming an Advocate for Transparent, Accountable, and Fair AI

DPOs must advocate for transparency in how AI systems use data, making sure that organizations disclose the purpose, scope, and data handling practices of AI models. This includes ensuring that the AI systems are explainable, so stakeholders can understand how decisions are made. Additionally, accountability means that the organization must take responsibility for the decisions and outcomes generated by AI systems, particularly in cases where AI models might impact individuals' rights or liberties.

- **Example: The European Union's GDPR and AI Regulation**: Under GDPR, organizations are required to ensure that AI decisions are transparent and explainable. DPOs at companies operating in the EU have a responsibility to

ensure these regulations are followed, promoting public trust in AI systems.
Website URL

Impact: By adhering to GDPR principles, companies not only ensure compliance but also help build public trust in their AI systems, fostering ethical data practices and reducing the potential for reputational harm.

---

3. Engaging with Stakeholders to Foster Public Trust in AI

DPOs have a critical role in engaging with internal and external stakeholders, including customers, regulatory bodies, and the general public. Engaging in open dialogues about AI's capabilities and limitations helps to foster trust. Regular updates, transparency in AI development, and clear communication regarding the safeguards in place to protect privacy are essential for ensuring that AI systems are seen as trustworthy by users and society.

- **Example: Microsoft's AI Ethics Committees**: Microsoft has established several ethics committees to assess AI models before they are deployed. DPOs within the company help facilitate this process by ensuring compliance with privacy laws and promoting responsible practices.
  Website URL

Impact: Engaging with stakeholders at all levels helps companies like Microsoft maintain a strong ethical framework, building trust in their AI solutions while ensuring that privacy is protected.

Action Point: Take Ownership and Lead in Promoting Responsible AI in Your Organization

To become a leader in AI ethics, DPOs must take a proactive stance. This involves setting clear ethical standards, working with cross-disciplinary teams to integrate data protection principles into the AI lifecycle, and engaging with external stakeholders to ensure that AI systems are transparent, accountable, and fair. By positioning themselves as ethical leaders within the organization, DPOs can foster a culture of responsibility around AI, ensuring that data protection and ethical considerations are front and center.

FAQ

Q1: How can DPOs lead the charge in AI ethics?
A1: DPOs can lead in AI ethics by setting clear guidelines for AI development, ensuring transparency in how AI systems use data, and advocating for accountability in AI-driven decisions. They should also work closely with legal, compliance, and AI development teams to ensure ethical standards are met.

Q2: Why is transparency in AI important for public trust?
A2: Transparency in AI helps users understand how their data is used and how decisions are made. By being transparent, organizations can build public trust in their AI systems, reduce fears about data misuse, and ensure compliance with data protection laws like GDPR.

Q3: What role does stakeholder engagement play in AI ethics?
A3: Engaging with stakeholders, including customers and regulators, is essential to building trust and ensuring that AI systems are ethical. Regular communication and collaboration ensure that ethical concerns are addressed, and that AI systems are deployed responsibly.

MOTD (Message of the Day)

"Be the change you want to see in AI — lead with ethics, responsibility, and transparency."

Chapter 11: Conclusion and Key Takeaways

11.4 The Path Forward for DPOs in AI Ethics

As AI technologies continue to advance and reshape industries, the responsibilities of Data Protection Officers (DPOs) are evolving. DPOs must prepare themselves to address emerging challenges, leverage new opportunities, and continuously adapt their strategies to protect data in the AI-driven future. This section explores how DPOs can stay ahead of the curve in AI ethics, ensuring both compliance and ethical governance of AI technologies.

---

1. The Evolving Responsibilities of the DPO as AI Technologies Advance

With the rapid growth of AI, the DPO's role is expanding beyond traditional data protection tasks to include ethical considerations surrounding the use of AI systems. The DPO will need to take an active role in guiding AI initiatives, ensuring that data protection principles such as privacy, fairness, and accountability are embedded from the design phase to deployment.

- **Example**: **IBM's AI Ethics and Data Protection Framework**: IBM has long been a leader in implementing AI ethics alongside data protection. Their DPOs play an essential role in ensuring that AI systems follow the company's ethical guidelines, balancing innovation with privacy protection. Website URL

Impact: By actively shaping AI initiatives with ethical guidelines, IBM minimizes the risk of AI bias and data misuse while creating systems that are transparent and accountable.

---

2. Preparing for Future Challenges and Opportunities in AI Ethics

DPOs must stay ahead of evolving AI regulations and anticipate potential challenges that may arise from AI's growing influence. The rapid pace of technological development, paired with a constantly shifting regulatory landscape, means DPOs must continuously update their knowledge and skills to adapt. This may involve upskilling in AI technology, participating in industry discussions, and staying informed about emerging ethical concerns such as algorithmic bias, transparency, and the societal impact of AI.

- **Example**: **The European Commission's AI Act**: The upcoming AI regulation from the EU aims to create a legal framework for AI use across Europe, addressing issues like risk assessment and transparency. DPOs in European companies will need to prepare for these changes by developing AI compliance strategies and ensuring that AI systems align with these new laws.

Impact: The AI Act will help shape how DPOs operate in the EU, ensuring that AI technologies are used responsibly and comply with rigorous data protection standards, protecting individuals' rights and privacy.

---

3. Building AI-Specific Data Protection Frameworks

As AI becomes more integrated into business operations, DPOs need to develop AI-specific data protection frameworks that address the unique risks and challenges posed by AI technologies. This framework should cover areas like data anonymization, algorithmic transparency, and decision-making processes, as well as the rights of individuals affected by AI-driven decisions. By creating these frameworks, DPOs can ensure that AI systems are ethically designed, transparent, and accountable.

- **Example**: **Salesforce's AI Ethics Framework**: Salesforce has created an AI ethics framework to guide its AI initiatives, ensuring that AI models are designed with privacy in mind and comply with ethical standards. Their DPOs work closely with AI teams to ensure that every AI solution meets data protection and ethical guidelines.

Impact: By establishing a strong framework, Salesforce ensures their AI models avoid biases and adhere to strict data protection standards, which not only protects privacy but also builds customer trust.

Action Point: Continuously Develop Your Expertise and Adapt Data Protection Strategies for AI

As AI technologies evolve, so too must the strategies and expertise of DPOs. Continuous professional development, staying updated with the latest regulatory changes, and collaborating with AI development teams will ensure that DPOs remain at the forefront of AI ethics. Regularly reviewing data protection frameworks, conducting risk assessments, and implementing AI-specific data protection strategies will enable DPOs to proactively address the ethical challenges that come with AI.

FAQ

Q1: What are the key responsibilities of DPOs as AI technologies advance?
A1: DPOs must evolve their roles by incorporating AI-specific data protection

frameworks, ensuring compliance with new regulations, guiding ethical AI practices, and monitoring the impact of AI on privacy and fairness throughout the AI lifecycle.

Q2: How can DPOs prepare for future challenges in AI ethics?
A2: DPOs can prepare by continuously developing their knowledge of emerging AI regulations, building expertise in AI technologies, and staying proactive in understanding new ethical concerns like algorithmic bias and the societal implications of AI.

Q3: Why is it important to build AI-specific data protection frameworks?
A3: AI-specific data protection frameworks are crucial for addressing the unique risks associated with AI, such as data misuse, algorithmic bias, and decision-making transparency. These frameworks help ensure that AI systems are both legally compliant and ethically responsible.

MOTD (Message of the Day)

"Embrace the future of AI with proactive leadership — continually evolve, stay informed, and lead with ethics."

Chapter 11: Conclusion and Key Takeaways

11.5 Final Thoughts and Conclusion

As artificial intelligence (AI) continues to grow and evolve, the role of the Data Protection Officer (DPO) becomes increasingly pivotal in guiding organizations toward ethical AI practices. In this final section, we will reflect on the DPO's critical responsibility in shaping the future of AI governance, the importance of leading with integrity, and the potential of AI to create a positive societal impact with proper oversight.

---

1. The DPO's Critical Role in Ensuring Ethical AI in a Rapidly Changing Landscape

The DPO plays a vital role in ensuring that AI systems are designed, deployed, and monitored with ethical considerations at their core. As AI technology evolves rapidly, it introduces new risks and challenges, such as algorithmic bias, data privacy concerns, and transparency issues. The DPO must stay vigilant, ensuring that AI initiatives adhere to data protection regulations like the **GDPR**, while also advocating for fairness, transparency, and accountability.

- **Example**: **Google's AI Ethics and Oversight**: Google has faced several challenges related to AI ethics, particularly with its AI research and deployment. The company's DPO has been instrumental in ensuring that AI projects align with privacy regulations and ethical principles, particularly after facing criticism over the use of facial recognition technology. Their role includes rigorous oversight of AI systems, ensuring compliance with data protection laws and ethical standards.
  Website URL

Impact: By leading the charge on ethical AI, Google has not only safeguarded users' data privacy but has also ensured that their AI systems are aligned with global ethical standards, fostering trust among users.

---

2. The Responsibility of DPOs to Lead with Integrity and Influence AI's Direction

DPOs must lead by example and influence the direction of AI development within their organizations. This involves fostering a culture of ethical decision-making and guiding AI teams to prioritize privacy, fairness, and non-discrimination. A proactive DPO should be involved from the early stages of AI project planning, offering guidance on ethical implications and ensuring that these issues are addressed throughout the project's lifecycle.

- **Example**: **Microsoft's Ethical AI Commitment**: Microsoft has embedded ethical AI principles into its organizational culture, with the DPO working closely with AI developers to ensure that AI technologies are built with a foundation of integrity. Their ethical AI policy emphasizes inclusivity, transparency, and accountability, with the DPO ensuring that these principles are upheld across all their AI-related projects.
  Website URL

Impact: Microsoft's approach to AI ethics ensures that AI systems are developed responsibly, minimizing risks such as bias or discrimination, while fostering public trust and regulatory compliance.

---

3. Looking Ahead: AI as a Tool for Positive Social Impact with the Right Ethical Oversight

AI has the potential to solve many of society's most pressing challenges, from healthcare to climate change. However, its ability to drive positive change depends on responsible governance. DPOs are at the forefront of ensuring that AI technologies are developed with ethical considerations that benefit society at large. By providing ethical oversight, DPOs can help shape AI as a tool for positive social impact, ensuring that its benefits are distributed fairly, and its risks mitigated.

- **Example**: **AI for Good Initiative by the UN**: The United Nations' AI for Good initiative leverages AI to address global issues, such as climate change, poverty, and health crises. DPOs in organizations participating in this initiative play an essential role in ensuring that AI solutions are deployed responsibly, protecting individual privacy while maximizing social benefits.
  Website URL

Impact: This initiative demonstrates how AI, when ethically managed, can drive transformative societal benefits, helping to address challenges such as healthcare access and environmental sustainability.

Action Point: Commit to Being a Leader in AI Data Ethics and Responsible Practices in the Future

The future of AI relies on responsible leadership in data ethics. As a DPO, you are uniquely positioned to influence how AI technologies are developed, ensuring that they respect fundamental rights, promote fairness, and maintain transparency. The call to action is clear: commit to leading your organization toward responsible, ethical AI practices. By continuously educating yourself, collaborating with AI teams, and advocating for ethical frameworks, you can ensure that AI is used as a force for good in society.

FAQ

Q1: What is the DPO's role in ensuring ethical AI?
A1: The DPO is responsible for ensuring that AI systems adhere to ethical standards and data protection regulations. This involves monitoring AI projects from the planning stage through deployment, advocating for privacy, fairness, and accountability, and ensuring compliance with laws like the GDPR.

Q2: How can DPOs influence AI development?
A2: DPOs influence AI development by offering ethical oversight, collaborating with AI teams, and ensuring that privacy and fairness are prioritized. They lead by example, ensuring that AI systems are transparent, inclusive, and non-discriminatory.

Q3: What are the benefits of ethical AI oversight?
A3: Ethical AI oversight fosters public trust, ensures compliance with regulations, minimizes risks such as bias and discrimination, and helps organizations leverage AI for positive societal impact, all while protecting privacy and individual rights.

MOTD (Message of the Day)

"Lead with integrity, shape the future of AI, and use technology to make the world a better place."

Summary

The Ethical AI Guide for DPO is an essential guide for Data Protection Officers (DPOs), privacy professionals, and anyone working with AI systems who wants to understand the intersection of data protection and artificial intelligence. In today's rapidly advancing digital landscape, where AI technologies are becoming integral to business operations, safeguarding data and ensuring ethical practices are more important than ever. This book provides a clear and comprehensive roadmap for DPOs to take a leadership role in AI ethics, helping organizations to maintain privacy and accountability while fostering innovation.

The book covers critical aspects of the DPO's responsibilities in managing AI-related data protection, such as understanding the ethical implications of AI, complying with global data protection regulations, and implementing frameworks that ensure the protection of personal and sensitive data. With an emphasis on practical advice and real-world examples, it helps readers understand how to navigate complex issues such as data breaches, transparency in AI algorithms, and the legal and ethical considerations involved in developing AI systems.

One of the key takeaways is the importance of integrating ethical considerations from the outset of AI development. As AI technologies continue to evolve, they bring with them new challenges in terms of data privacy, security, and bias. *The Ethical AI Guide for DPO* highlights the proactive role that DPOs can play in ensuring that AI systems are designed with privacy, fairness, and transparency in mind. The book outlines effective strategies for DPOs to collaborate with AI development teams, advocate for ethical practices, and establish an AI ethics framework within their organization.

Additionally, the book delves into real-world case studies, demonstrating both successes and failures in AI data protection. These examples provide valuable insights into how DPOs can influence AI policies, avoid common pitfalls, and drive a culture of responsibility and continuous improvement. Readers will also find guidance on how to prepare for future trends and challenges in AI and data protection, ensuring that they stay ahead of the curve in an ever-evolving field.

By the end of the book, readers will have a deeper understanding of how AI technologies impact data privacy and protection and will be equipped with the tools and knowledge necessary to become key players in the responsible development and deployment of AI. Whether you're a beginner or an intermediate professional in the field of data protection, this book serves as a comprehensive and practical resource to help you lead with confidence and ethical responsibility in the age of AI.

The Ethical AI Guide for DPO is more than just a book; it's a call to action for data protection professionals to embrace their critical role in shaping the future of AI in a responsible, transparent, and ethical manner.

Action & Way Forward

The Ethical AI Guide for DPO equips Data Protection Officers (DPOs) and privacy professionals with the knowledge and tools to lead ethical AI initiatives within organizations. To harness the power of AI while ensuring data privacy and protection, it's essential to take proactive steps toward integrating ethics and data protection principles into every AI-related decision. Below are the key action points and ways forward for DPOs:

1. **Establish Clear AI Ethics Frameworks**

   o **Action**: Develop and implement a robust AI ethics framework tailored to your organization's needs, ensuring that AI systems are transparent, fair, and respect privacy.

   o **Way Forward**: Continuously review and adapt this framework in response to emerging AI technologies and regulatory changes. Build a living document that reflects ethical considerations in every AI deployment.

2. **Collaborate with AI Development Teams**

   o **Action**: Position yourself as a trusted advisor within AI development teams, ensuring ethical and legal considerations are front-and-center throughout the design and deployment phases.

   o **Way Forward**: Foster cross-functional collaboration between data protection officers, data scientists, engineers, and legal teams. This will enable you to catch potential issues early and align AI models with ethical standards.

3. **Embrace Proactive Compliance & Risk Assessment**

   o **Action**: Regularly conduct risk assessments and audits to ensure AI systems comply with data protection laws such as GDPR, CCPA, and others. This helps identify vulnerabilities and mitigate privacy risks before they materialize.

   o **Way Forward**: Implement a continuous compliance strategy. As AI technologies evolve rapidly, DPOs should stay updated with the latest regulatory changes and be prepared to address them swiftly.

4. **Drive Ethical AI in Your Organization**

   o **Action**: Be an advocate for fairness, transparency, and accountability in AI practices. Work to eliminate bias and ensure that AI systems do not discriminate against certain groups of individuals.

- o **Way Forward**: Lead by example and champion AI ethics within the organization. Host workshops, training sessions, and awareness campaigns to educate teams about the ethical implications of AI.

5. **Monitor and Review AI Systems Regularly**

   - o **Action**: Ensure that there are ongoing monitoring mechanisms in place for AI systems once they are live. Regular reviews are crucial to detect any unintended consequences or privacy breaches early.

   - o **Way Forward**: Set up automated systems for monitoring AI decisions and outcomes. Introduce feedback loops that allow for rapid response and corrective actions if ethical or legal issues arise.

6. **Prepare for Future AI Challenges**

   - o **Action**: Anticipate the future challenges posed by AI technologies in terms of data privacy and ethics. Start building scalable and adaptable solutions now to prepare for new regulations, advanced AI models, and unforeseen ethical dilemmas.

   - o **Way Forward**: Develop a roadmap for your organization's AI ethics strategy, outlining long-term goals, timelines, and responsible AI use. Stay ahead of the curve by continuously engaging with evolving AI trends and policy developments.

7. **Foster International Cooperation**

   - o **Action**: Monitor global AI governance trends and data protection regulations to ensure compliance across regions. Collaborate with international peers to share insights and best practices.

   - o **Way Forward**: Engage in industry groups and forums dedicated to AI ethics. This will help you stay informed about cross-border regulations, and facilitate more effective data protection strategies.

By following these action points, DPOs can become catalysts for ethical AI development within their organizations. The future of AI lies in its responsible and ethical deployment, and as a DPO, you have the critical responsibility to ensure that AI technologies serve humanity positively while safeguarding individual privacy rights. *The Ethical AI Guide for DPO* offers the roadmap—now it's time to act and lead the way forward.

Feedback Request

The author kindly requests your feedback on the written book and its contents to enhance its quality and effectiveness. Your insights are invaluable in driving improvement and ensuring the information presented is as beneficial as possible.

Please share your thoughts and suggestions by reaching out via email at
Ravi.R.Info@Gmail.com

Your contribution is greatly appreciated and will play a significant role in the ongoing development of this work. Thank you for your support!

Thank You 🙏